Alternative Dimension
the shield of Excalibur

T R Eden

chipmunkapublishing
the mental health publisher

TR Eden

Published by
Chipmunkapublishing
United Kingdom

http://www.chipmunkapublishing.com

Copyright © 2016 T R EDen

ISBN   978-1-78382-314-7

Alternative Dimension 2

Introduction

It had taken Derek (head of a yellow cat, purple wings, and a humanoid body covered in orange) around two months to create enough living metal to copy the school and village on board the new space craft, which was now capable of jumping to any dimension. Since the encounter with the Evil Lord, they had stayed one step ahead by dimension jumping.

Mr Shaw (looked human, but had a dinosaurs' body and fly-like eyes) was in his office. His crystal ball started to glow, requesting him to answer. He thought this was very strange. As the head teacher of the school, he was not that important. The crystal ball glowed orange, which meant it was a priority message from the witches. The ball then cleared, to show a human woman with blonde hair and blue eyes.

"Good to see you again," she said.

Mr Shaw looked shocked – he had never met this person before.

"It's me, Devena, Queen of the witches," she said. She looked worried, which was unusual as she was normally full of confidence. "I have contacted you because I have a mission for you and your students. I want you to get me the Shield of Excalibur."

"What's that?" Mr Shaw asked.

"It is a magical item that will help me to weaken the Evil Lord's powers. I will give you the details of the dimension you need to transfer to."

"Why have I never heard about the shield?" Mr Shaw asked.

"It's locked away in another dimension, an alternative reality to the one that you know. Dimensions are like railway tracks, and you posses the only ship that can break these barriers."

TR Eden

Mr Shaw was really angry. He pointed out that he had told the students he would not put them in danger again, which had calmed them down, especially our three heroes. Max (blond hair, blue eyes, black and yellow tenth level wizards' cloths) suffered from OCD, which meant he was constantly checking things and organising his property; Jack (spiked blond hair, green eyes, tenth level robe) saw horrific images; and finally Alison (brown hair, green eyes, 10th level robe), whose problem was anxiety.

Mr Shaw asked, "Is there another way, instead of endangering the children again?"

Devena shook her head, and pointed out that the Evil Lord was able to travel across dimensions a lot better than she could. If he ever got hold of the shield he would become even more powerful. Mr Shaw reluctantly agreed, knowing that he would have to break the news to his students. Knowing of Max, Jack and Alison's needs, he decided to tell them in private first.

Jack's images were quite stable until he heard the news. Then the visions of what might happen in the future kicked in. Alison was so taken with fright she could not move, and Max ran over to the sink to make sure all the items on it were in exactly the same place that he had left them.

Mr Shaw said, "If it helps in the battle with the Evil Lord we have to try and help. I will need your help on this mission because, although this will be a different version of it, this is your home planet, so you will understand how things work better than us."

"What do you mean by a different dimension?" asked Jack.

Mr Shaw explained about dimensions and opposite dimensions; basically an opposite dimension is mostly the same with a few changes.

They prepared the ship for dimensional transport. The chosen ones and Derek had discovered a root to the dimension they wanted. There was, however, a problem. To

Alternative Dimension 2

get to the right dimension they would have to cross several other dimensions. To get there, the ship could only safely cross one dimension at a time.

Mr Shaw called a meeting with all the students in the school's great hall, to tell them what to expect when they crossed dimensions. He said that the ship would bend and creak, due to the amount of stress being placed on it.

All the students looked scared and frightened, especially Max, Jack, and Alison. After all, they were only tenth level wizards, and so were their class mates. They were Jade (spiky orange fur on her head, brown fur on her body); Dylan/Coby (a conjoined life form with green skin and yellow eyes, they had two heads with two brains that were linked by telepathy); Sam (a blob of yellow, organic material); Hailey (red skin, large ears and purple tail); and finally Kim (black eyes, orange skin, brown fur).

They could hear the ship starting to bend and rattle, like there was a tremendous earth quake. Mr Shaw ordered all the students to their dormitories. He asked if Max, Jack and Alison could stay in his office, where he performed a localised gravity spell. The room stopped shaking straight away. He asked what he could do to make the mission easier.

Alison's mind was full of worry and stress. All Jack could see were people dying all over again. Max was pacing up-and-down, thinking he had left a tap turned on somewhere. They had a talk between themselves, then said that they would go willingly on one condition – that their classmates were allowed to come with them. They did not trust anyone else, given the fact that they had descended from a race of people that hunted witches. Mr Shaw reluctantly agreed to the term.

As the ship started to cross into the right dimension, Mr Shaw used his crystal ball to get a look at the country, so he would be able to show it to Alison, Max and Jack. They nervously looked at the crystal ball.

"This does not look like our Britain," Alison explained, "It's a completely different shape."

Jack looked stunned, "Where is Scotland?"

Max pointed out that, in this dimension, it looked like Scotland was a separate island.

Mr Shaw was so shocked about what he had been told by the three students, he summoned Devena. She told him that this was Britain in some ways, the same as Max, Jack and Alison remembered it, and in other ways it was completely different.

"It is an alternative dimension," Devena explained, "In this reality, England and Wales are made up of small Kingdoms across the country. The most powerful of these Kingdoms is Camelot. I will provide directions when you land."

Mr Shaw asked if Mr Underwood (head like a jellyfish, a light-green feathered body with a touch of yellow skin) could come to his office.

Mr Shaw asked Mr Underwood if he would escort the children to Camelot.

Mr Underwood was shocked to be offered this mission, and said he wanted no part of it. However, Mr Shaw convinced him that they would need someone they trusted. Being one of their teachers, he would be reassuring.

"But how are we going to get there? We don't look like humans."

Mr Shaw smiled. "I want you and the students to report to the chosen ones straight away."

The chosen ones insisted that Max, Jack, Alison and Prex should go after all. Max, Jack and Alison were humans, and Prex could easily shed his skin and take on a human form.

Alternative Dimension 2

"But for the rest of you, we will have to perform a camouflage spell."

This was difficult, because the spell required constant concentration, which is why only a small group could go on this mission.

They had converted everyone except Dylan /Coby, who insisted they wanted to go on the mission. The chosen ones pointed out that there are no co-joined life forms on earth. The only way they could go would be for them to merge into one being, with one head. Dylan /Coby talked about this for a minute telepathically. They came to the conclusion that, as they are linked telepathically, they would easily be able to cope with one head.

After the transformation, the group were Jade (now had long blonde hair, blue eyes, 5ft 11, wearing cloths made out of pure gold), Dylan /Coby (became a male, 6ft, dressed as a Knight, with one head which had brown hair and blue eyes, solid steal armour with Jade's crest on it, their minds had become one), Sam (was also a Knight with the same suit of armour, black hair, brown eyes and was 6ft 1), Hailey (had become an advisor to the crown, long, ginger hair with blue eyes, about 5ft 10 she wore the robes of state which were red silk with gold trimmings, her pretend job was to advise Jade when possible), Kim (was transformed into the keeper of the texts – this was basically a librarian who had the important task of guarding some magic texts – she was 5ft 9, short black hair, brown eyes and was dressed in civilian clothes which were brown trousers, black jacket and a blue cape of office), Mr Underwood (disguised as Jade's personal servant, short yellow hair, brown eyes, 6 foot tall and was dressed in servant's robes which were basically posh standard clothes, he had black trousers and jacket with a white shirt), Prex (could change into any shape) and Max, Jack and Alison (dressed in standard peasant clothes: brown trousers and jackets, dirty white shirts).

The group left the ship and headed for Camelot. To gain access through other Kingdoms, the chosen ones had suggested they should pretend to be a royal party, with Jade acting as the Princess, as she was so confident talking to complete strangers.

Alternative Dimension 2

Inside Camelot

Uther, the old King (tall at 5ft 9, blue eyes, short blond hair, wears the royal robes of Camelot and a gold crown), was dying. His son Arthur (6ft, well-built, long blond hair, blue eyes, wore the Prince's uniform which had the emblem of Camelot stitched in pure gold thread), was trying to make his father more comfortable by distracting him. He talked about trade routes with other Kingdoms.

Merlin (when in human-form he appears as an old man with a long white beard), was the King's Chief medicine man and closest friend. He entered the room, asking if he could have a word with Arthur.

He said, "There may be a medicine that we have not tried yet."

Arthur looked up and asked him to explain.

"It temporarily relives stress and pain from the patient, but only lasts 48 hours. Then there is nothing else we can do."

"Why can't he take another dose after 48 hours?" Arthur asked.

Merlin explained that the medicine was actually also a poison. If you take too much you will die painfully.

Arthur wanted to spend as much time as possible with his father. He walked into the Great Hall. There, eating their lunch, were the Knights of Camelot. Arthur fetched his six friends from their lunch. They were Sir Gawain (5ft 10, ginger hair, brown eyes, wears the armour of Camelot); Sir Galahad (6ft, brown eyes, long brown hair, wears the armour of Camelot); Sir Lancelot du Lake (6ft, long blond hair, green eyes, wears the armour of Camelot); Sir Ector (5ft 11, ginger hair, brown eyes, wears the armour of Camelot); Sir Melligrance (6ft, green eyes, blond hair, wears the armour of Camelot); Sir Gaheris (6ft, blond hair, blue eyes, wears the armour of Camelot).

TR Eden

Arthur had been told by Merlin of the two items he needed for the medicine, so Arthur sent his Knights out to collect them. The first item was bear hair, which had to be collected from a giant British bear.

The Knights were worried. They did not mind taking on an invading army, but an 11 foot bear was another matter.

Sir Ector and Sir Galahad picked up the scent straight away. They were able to do this because, when away from Camelot, they had to track their own food.

Sir Galahad led them to a section of the wood where they found a sleeping bear. They could not believe their luck! Sir Gawain tip-toed quietly towards the bear, but a twig broke under his foot. The bear sprung into life. He charged Sir Melligrance. Sir Gawain ordered them to grab their swords.

Sir Galahad said, "Are you crazy? We cannot perform hand-to-hand combat on a bear!"

Sir Gawain asked if they had a better idea. Then they noticed that some bear fur had been caught on a bramble. Whilst Sir Lancelot ran over to grab it, the others formed a circle around him. He grabbed the fur, but the bear did nothing. They turned around and saw some cubs. He was obviously protecting them.

The next ingredient was unicorn blood. These were peaceful and timid creatures, which had been hunted close to extinction. Their blood contained a chemical which stops ageing.

When they tracked down the scent of the unicorns, they were all shocked. Someone had killed a baby unicorn and left it for dead. They collected a sample of its blood.

They started to head back to Camelot, when they bumped into the school party, which now looked completely human. Mr Underwood started to explain that they were a small part of Princess Jade's court, and that they were on their way to pay respect to the King.

Alternative Dimension 2

Sir Galahad said, "The King is in no state to receive visitors, he is gravely ill."

Mr Underwood asked if they could make an exception.

The Knights had a talk amongst themselves.

"Very well," Sir Gawain said, "We will escort you to the Prince Arthur, and it will be his decision whether Uther sees you or not."

The chosen ones were watching the events through the students they were camouflaging. They summoned Derek to come to their chambers.

Abby wondered aloud "If we are pretending to have a Kingdom, can we use the living metal to form an island? It's easier for us to concentrate if we are in touch with the ground," she said.

Derek said, "Certainly," and did it straight away.

The party arrived in Camelot, and Arthur had his Guard rush upstairs straight away with the items.

Arthur rushed into the King's chamber and handed the items to Merlin, then ordered the court to leave him in peace. He claimed it was hard to make the medicine, and he needed to be alone to concentrate. The real reason was that he was going to use magic to help. Uther had banned magic, thinking it was evil, but Merlin was a white sorcerer. He only used magic for good. If Uther had found out what he was doing he would have locked him up for ten years.

Merlin was desperate to save the King's life. He mixed the items together. Merlin's witchcraft was quite weak, which was why he wanted the unicorn blood, for it amplifies magical energy.

He performed the incantation. The potion started to boil as he was holding it. Merlin gave it to Uther, and he slowly came round.

"Thank you old friend," he said.

Arthur came rushing into his Dad's chambers, and thanked Merlin for all his help.

Merlin reminded Arthur that the potion would only last 48 hours.

"After that there is nothing I can do," he said.

Uther welcomed the students. At Jade's court he asked her where her country of origin was.

She turned to Mr Underwood who replied, "It's just off the coast, close to Cornwall."

The chosen ones had performed a piece of telepathy to tell Mr Underwood that the ship was now an island.

Uther looked surprised. He did not know of an island in that location.

Merlin sensed they had magical powers, and decided to support their story by saying that he knew of an island in that location.

Uther explained that he had two Kingdoms, one which was Camelot, and the other a collection of land above Camelot called 'the Other-land'. Due to the amount of control it took to rule two Kingdoms, the Other-land always went to the second in-line, which would be Arthur.

"However I want him to take over Camelot when I die, so his half-sister Morgan rules the Other-land," Uther said.

After they had eaten dinner, Merlin escorted the students to his apartment and said he felt that they had magical powers. Mr Underwood asked if they could trust him.

Alternative Dimension 2

Meanwhile, Max was convinced he had forgotten to do something, and was pacing up-and-down. Alison was so anxious she had to take deep breaths to calm down, and all Jack could see were horrible things that can't be described.

Jack asked Merlin, "Why is England much bigger than our dimension, and why is the layout of the country completely different?"

Merlin explained, "You have answered your own question. This is an alternative Britain from the one you came from."

"How do you know we are from a different dimension?" Mr Underwood asked.

Merlin replied, "Because your camouflage magic does not totally work on me. I can see dimensional energy surrounding you like a residual substance, which you collect when you jump dimension."

Merlin looked at the students. "There is a lot of magical potential inside your students, but no way to direct that power."

Merlin pressed a button underneath his desk. All of a sudden a book case appeared in the corner of the room. Merlin used magic to scan the contents of the books. He searched through hundreds of books in one minute. He was able to scan the contents using magic, by holding a hand over the front cover and concentrating. Eventually he came across what he was looking for. He was going to teach them a spell which would allow the students to transfer their magical potential through their wands, and direct it on to Mr Underwood.

Most of the group did this with ease; however Jack, Alison and Max were having trouble concentrating on the spell, especially Jack who had violent and aggressive thoughts. Merlin told the three heroes that they must try to focus, and try to cope with what was going on inside their heads.

Max was still worried about his wand. He kept on thinking he had left it behind. He constantly checked his pockets for it, when he actually had it on him the whole time. Alison was so nervous she kept on remembering what had happened to her friends back in Antarctica, and Jack's images were racing. But somehow they were able to focus for a few minutes. They pointed their wands at Mr Underwood and were able to transfer their energy to him. Then a blast of energy from Mr Underwood's wand shot out, sending him backwards and on to the floor.

Merlin congratulated the students and Mr Underwood. Max, Jack and Alison felt guilty because they could only transfer their powers for five minutes. Mr Underwood took them to one side and said he did not blame them.

"I feel so useless," Max said.

Jack was having trouble controlling his guilt, and Alison was in tears saying "We let you down" over and over again.

Mr Underwood told them it was not their fault. "You can't be expected to cope with every situation you come across. Just try your best in everything you do and that's good enough for me."

Now that everyone in the group could perform the spell, Merlin went to see Uther. He asked if Jade and her court could join the Camelot Council. This was the central parliament. Merlin pointed out that they could be a great use to the realm.

Uther agreed. He had learnt a long time ago that Merlin had a gift for judging people. He was hardly ever wrong. Merlin's real motive though, was to use the student's powers if needed.

Uther said, "As long as they don't posses any magical abilities which could threaten the council."

Merlin lied in a firm voice and said, "I can give you that promise."

Alternative Dimension 2

The Story of the Shield

That evening, the students and Mr Underwood went to see Merlin to ask about the Shield of Excalibur. As soon as they asked him about the shield he started to shake with fear.

"How do you know about the shield?" he replied. "Only a few people know that it exists. How did you find out about it?"

Mr Underwood explained that the witch Queen, who could see across other dimensions, said that she needed the shield to help in the battle with the Evil Lord, and that whatever happened not to allow him to have it because it would amplify his powers.

Merlin could not believe what he was hearing. The idea that anyone from another dimension knew of the shield worried him greatly. He decided to explain how the shield was created. Merlin started to explain.

"The greatest student I ever had was Morgan".

Max interrupted with shock. "Arthur's half sister? How could that be possible? You said magic was banned from the Kingdoms of Camelot."

Merlin continued, "We practised in secret. And we were not the only ones. There were lots of so-called magic cults over the whole of the island, including Kingdoms of Camelot."

Mr Underwood tried to bring the conversation back to the shield by asking how powerful she now was. Merlin told him that she had become the most powerful black sorcerer he had ever met.

"She wanted to use magic for herself rather than others," he explained. "It was on the last night before she was due to leave to take control of the Other-land, because Uther had commanded it to happen after he died. Also he did not totally trust her loyalty to her brother Arthur.

TR Eden

"A massive shooting star crashed into a field outside Camelot. The explosion was so loud it made the ground shake. Morgan and I wanted to be the first people to see what it was, so we performed transport magic. When we arrived at the point of impact there was a glowing orange metal inside a massive crater. We had never seen anything like it before. As we both ran over to grab it, the metal somehow absorbed our powers so it was 50% white magic and 50% black magic.

"But what I discovered was that the edges were quite flexible, so when it cooled down I was able to bend it into the shape of a shield."

"Then what did you do with it?" Mr Underwood asked.

Merlin continued. "I used all my magic to block Morgan sensing the shield's powers, but I could only do this for a short period of time, so I needed to hide it somewhere where Morgan could not feel its energy calling her. So I gave it to my best friend, the lady of the lake."

Then Merlin told the students that it was time to go to bed.

Whilst they were asleep, a loud bell rang around midnight, and a messenger called out "The King is dead."

The announcement sent a shiver down Merlin's back. He knew that he had done everything possible for the King.

The announcement unnerved Max, who constantly checked that the taps were off in their room in Camelot castle. Alison was frozen with fright, and all Jack could visualise were horrible images. They came running up to Mr Underwood, who was able to calm them down. They did not react well when the future was uncertain.

Alternative Dimension 2

Uther's Funeral

Funeral rights in Camelot were complicated when it came to the death of a King. The first part of the ritual was for the King's most trusted Knights to get down on one knee and tell a story that showed respect for the dead King. Sir Gaheris started by telling a story about a hunt and the King's excellent tracking skills.

"We followed a wild stag deep into the forest and caught it, but we were lost inside the forest without a trained tracker or guide. As it was becoming a cold night, a cold wind started to blow through the forest and we started to shake with cold. Then Uther took command and, using only the moonlight, he was able to lead us back to Camelot."

Sir Ector was the next Knight to speak. His memory of the King was a trade mission to establish a trade route between Camelot and the merchant ports of the South.

"Negotiations were difficult because the merchants wanted gold in return for the use of their ports. Uther knew if he gave them the amount of gold they wanted Camelot would be broke. Uther came up with a counter offer. Everyone knew that the Camelot guard were the most loyal troops in the known world. Instead of gold, he said he would give them twenty of my finest troops to defend their ports and stop smugglers from stealing the contents from cargo ships and selling the cargo on the black market."

The next to speak was Sir Gareth. He said that, "It was Uther who founded the code of Camelot, which says that no-one in the land is more important than anyone else. Leaders show respect for their followers and followers show respect for their leaders."

The next ritual was to have some paintings made of the King. These painters were commissioned by the King. He had hand-picked the best twenty painters he could find. They would paint him after his death.

TR Eden

Under Camelot law, no-one but the chosen people could look directly at the King's body. The rest of the subjects would pay their respects by going to their community halls. These were buildings designed to allow the community to gather and chat about anything, from news or what they were doing that day.

Merlin went to supervise the work on the paintings. He pointed out that, although they were painting the King after his death, the pictures should be adapted to show the King as he used to be when he was younger.

The paintings were finished after a couple of days work and taken to the community halls. The people flocked to see the pictures and lay pink roses before the picture.

Arthur did not sleep that night because he was upset about his father, but also because he would be King of Camelot and the Other-land. He asked Merlin to join him. He told Merlin about his doubts in his ability to rule the Kingdom as well as his father had.

Merlin replied, "You should have more faith in yourself."

Alternative Dimension 2

The Day of the Funeral

Arthur invited the students to attend the funeral dressed as Jade and her court. Mr Underwood told Jade to accept the invitation on behalf of the group. Max, Jack and Alison did not want to go. They hated crowded situations. They kept thinking everyone must be watching them.

Merlin arrived to talk to the group.

"The rituals of the island state that each King is entitled to call themselves King within their own Kingdom. If they visit another Kingdom, their title becomes Prince, because that Kingdom has its own King."

"Why are you telling us this?" Mr Underwood asked.

Merlin smiled. "I am telling you this because, when other Kingdoms arrive at Camelot, they are to be treated as if they are Kings of the country they are in."

Mr Underwood said, "Jade is very polite."

Merlin pointed out that, in their fake court, Jade was the only one with Royal status. "The rest are noble men who have to address Kings and Queens properly."

Jack was uneasy about the funeral because he hated death, given what had happened to his friends in Antarctica. All he could see were dead people in front of him, which made him feel like there was a cold chill running down his spine.

Alison had the same problem. Her anxiety was so extreme that she found it difficult to focus on anything else, and Max was so anxious that he was checking his pockets every 30 seconds, to make sure he had not dropped anything.

The funeral started at the Town Hall. The bells inside the Kingdom were ringing as the Guard of Camelot marched from the Royal apartments into the town. Following the guard came the coffin, made out of pure gold, and carried by the King's knights.

TR Eden

The people rushed into the streets to pay their respects to a good leader. The coffin was taken to its final resting place in the Royal temple, where the private service took place. Arthur and the rest of the selected people joined him. Morgan was invited but chose not to attend, given her father's attitude towards magic.

As a matter of respect at the end of the service, Arthur had to take an oath of Kingship, promising to defend the Kingdoms and look after the people he would rule. The head of the service took the crown from Uther's body and gave it to Arthur, the official King of Camelot and the Other-land.

That night they had the traditional feast to celebrate and remember. The whole court exchanged stories with each other to remember the past King, and they celebrated Arthur as the new King.

The ladies of Camelot were flirting with Arthur, knowing whoever he decided to marry would become Queen of Camelot. Arthur said he felt tired and wanted to go back to his courtiers. He asked if Merlin could join him.

Arthur said anxiously, "I don't think I am going to make a good King."

Merlin shook his head. "That's nonsense. I helped bring you up. I know you can do this Arthur."

Arthur said, "If only there was a way to be sure."

"How do you mean?" Merlin asked.

"Just a sign to show that I am the true leader of Camelot and the Other-land."

Merlin then told Arthur about a sword in a stone, and that only a true King can remove it. Arthur said he would set up a Royal guard party to hunt for the sword in the stone.

Merlin went to warn the students about what was going to happen. He pointed out that he may need them to use their

Alternative Dimension 2

magical strength to protect Arthur. Mr Underwood was furious! Merlin had told them that magic was banned from Camelot and they would go to prison for practicing it.

Merlin smiled. "Just use it when no one is looking."

"How?" Mr Underwood asked.

Merlin gave an example."If there was a fire blocking our path, you could help me make it rain to put it out. I am also worried about Morgan."

Mr Underwood asked why?

Merlin pointed out that she was dangerous.

"She is obsessed with power and would love the throne of Camelot, and would use her army to attack Arthur."

Mr Underwood was confused. "She does not have an army. She rules the Other-land in the name of Arthur."

"There are two problems with that," Merlin said worryingly. "The first is that the Other-land has been controlled separately for 400 years. It is practically independent from Camelot with its own traditions and laws. If they thought we were going to take that away from them they would attack us.

"And secondly, Morgan is their most popular Queen for centuries."

TR Eden

The Sword in the Stone

The next day, Arthur's bodyguards mounted their horses in the castle courtyard. The head of the guard (5ft 11, dirty black/blue eyes, wore the servant's guard uniform) went into the castle to tell him they were ready.

Arthur was having a last minute talk with his favourite Knights.

Sir Gawain said, "If you doubt your ability to be a great King, then you have to come on the quest. If Merlin was right, the enchanted sword belongs to you, the true King of Camelot."

The other Knights made similar comments, and they all agreed it was the right thing to do.

Sir Melligrance advised caution. If the trip would take them through the land controlled by witch tribes, they would gladly kill Arthur because of the way his father treated them. Arthur said he would be careful, but that the benefits out-weighed the risk.

Merlin insisted that the students should go along. They would be able to generate extra magical energy. They were still pretending to be a court from another island. Mr Underwood went off to tell the students about their next mission.

Prex was looking forward to the chance to go on a quest with Merlin, probably one of the greatest sorcerers of all time. Max, Jack and Alison wanted to go back to the ship where it was safer. Mr Underwood took them to one side and reminded them of their mission. Did they want the Evil Lord to have the shield and threaten everyone else with it? Jack pointed out that the Evil Lord did not know about the shield. Mr Underwood pointed out that he can cross dimensions with ease. If he did know about it he would try to get it.

Jack, Max and Alison had a conversation between themselves. After a few minutes discussing the problem they

Alternative Dimension 2

reluctantly agreed to help. They hated the way the Evil Lord killed people by stealing their ability to think for themselves. Mr Underwood told the students that sometimes we have to try and face our fears, even if we don't want to.

The group went into the courtyard where Arthur was waiting. Arthur smiled at Jade.

"As you are a Royal court, I have provided you with some of my best horses."

They all mounted their horse and prepared to set off.

The guard of the gate shouted, "Open the gate for the King of Camelot and Princess Jade."

The party passed through the gates and headed for the dark forest, which was in the middle of land occupied by the witch tribes. Arthur had a chat with Mr Underwood who was pretending to be Jade's bodyguard. Arthur asked him how long he had served Princess Jade. He lied and said about two years. He then asked Arthur a question.

"Why is your father hated by the magical people of the island?"

Arthur shook his head. He was ashamed of what his father had done.

"He thought all forms of magic were unnatural. He drove out the people who could perform magic and banished them to other kingdoms. If they were found to posses magic but did not declare it, they were imprisoned in the castle dungeon.

"He hunted magical creatures. The ones he hurt the most were the dragons. My father thought they were evil because they were such ancient creatures. He believed it was impossible that anything with such a long life-span could possibly be good."

Merlin overheard the conversation and said, "That's not the end of the story. Before the Dragon King left, he breathed fire onto a sword and smashed it into a giant piece of rock. That's what we have come to collect."

Arthur was shocked, and asked Merlin, "After what my father has done, how can I be the one to pull out the sword?"

Merlin said simply, "Because you are not your father."

The group marched into the forest when, all of a sudden, an arrow almost hit Arthur in the shoulder. The Knights formed a circle around their King.

Suddenly a man jumped out from behind a tree and said, "I see you have gold and I want to take it."

He was a highway man (scruffy clothes; a brown shirt with ripped, brown trousers, dark-brown hair and blue eyes).

Arthur emerged from the centre of the circle and said, "Do you know who I am?"

The man fell to the floor and begged for forgiveness. Arthur said, "Do you know that for endangering my life you are looking at a prison term of 50 years?"

The man started to shake. Arthur asked him if he know the area well.

"Yes my King," he replied.

Arthur had a chat with Merlin. Arthur said that he was tempted to make the man a counter offer, if he agreed to be their guide and help them to miss the witches' campsites.

"I will grant him a pardon and allow him to go with a warning instead," Merlin said. "That makes complete sense. If we go through the forest without a guide and end up in a large radical witch camp, they would want to take us prisoner because of the way your father persecuted them."

What they did not realise was that there was a witch-tribe camp less than a mile away from them, who were watching

Alternative Dimension 2

the progress of the group by using a short- range sight potion. Inside the camp itself, there had to be at least a hundred witches. They were constantly informing the head witch of the village. This was an old lady (she had a humped back, a long nose, poor eyesight, brown eyes, brown hair, and was dressed in the head of the witch tribe robes).

She asked the witches that were monitoring the group, "Where are they?"

"The party searching for the dragon's breath sword in-the-stone is extremely close to our camp. They are being guided by a highway man," one of the witches said (blue eyes, brown hair, dressed in the robes of servants to the head witch).

She continued, "As they are so close, maybe we should capture Arthur. We would go down in history as the witches who performed justice for our people."

The witch pointed out, "If we did capture Arthur, we would be hunted down by a combined army from most of the kingdoms on the island. It would be a battle we would be unable to win."

The tribe agreed. As long as Arthur did not violate their tribal land they would let him pass through the forest. They would, however, keep on watching him, using sight potion.

The highway man led the royal party to a cave. The entrance was blocked. Arthur thanked the highway man and gave him his freedom.

There was a giant waterfall flowing, but it was not water, it was fire. Then a large voice came echoing from the cave.

"To make the fires go out you must answer the riddle of Kings. Who is more important, the King or the subject?"

Arthur spent thirty minutes thinking about it. Then it came to him. If he said the King he would be power-mad. If he said the subject it would mean that he puts people first, making him a good King. So he said the subject.

The waterfall of fire opened to reveal a pathway. The voice spoke again.

"Only one subject may come with you into the cave, so pick your most trusted servant."

Arthur picked Merlin and they both entered the cave together.

Inside the cave was a massive area. In front of them was a river made of a substance which they had never seen before. It looked like a lake of liquid gold. Then, all of a sudden, the sword appeared from the ground, encased in crystal and stone.

Arthur asked Merlin, "How do we cross it?"

Then the voice replied, "You have to prove that you are from Royal blood."

Merlin thought about it for five minutes then clicked his fingers. He told Arthur to prick his finger with a knife.

"Now what?" Arthur asked.

Merlin said, "Hold your finger out in front of you."

A drop of blood fell into the river and a stepping stone appeared. Merlin tried it first to see if it was safe. Arthur then repeated this over and over again, until he had a stepping stone path to the sword.

Arthur asked his friend, "How do I pull it out?"

Merlin smiled. "Just hold your hand out over it."

The sword sprung into his hand.

Alternative Dimension 2

When they came out of the cave and saw Arthur holding the sword, everyone got down on one knee and said, "Hail to the true King of Camelot."

Battle Plan

On the way back to the castle, Merlin told Arthur about the shield, but chose to tell it as a pretend myth so as not to alarm him. He did not mention how his sister was involved in the creation of it.

Arthur was shocked. He could not understand how Merlin, his most trusted companion, would have any knowledge of magical forces, especially given how his father believed that all magic was evil.

Merlin knew that if he had confessed to having magical abilities, Uther would have had him locked up in prison. Merlin wanted some advice on magical matters, so he went to have a conversation with Mr Underwood, who knew nothing about this planet or the people evolved. So reluctantly he asked Max, Jack and Alison for advice.

Max was walking up and down, thinking he was sure he had left his draws unlocked in his dormitory. Alison was so anxious she kept on thinking that the worst was going to happen; that they would be captured and imprisoned. Jack's images were horrific. However they tried their best to advise Merlin.

Jack pointed out, "You are King Arthur's most trusted advisor and he trusted you to use your powers to protect the kingdom."

Merlin thanked the students for their help.

That evening, Merlin was going to explain everything to King Arthur and his friends. He sat them down by a fire.

When they had settled down, Merlin said, "My friends, I have a shock for you, so you better brace yourselves."

"What is it?" Gawain asked.

"I am a white sorcerer."

Alternative Dimension 2

Arthur was stunned. "But you were my father's most trusted friend."

Merlin smiled. "I only use my powers for good. Uther believed all magic was evil, where, in actual fact, it's down to the person how they choose to use it."

Arthur said he would have to think about what he was going to do with him.

Merlin continued, "Here comes the most shocking part. My student was someone with a strong magical ability, your half sister Morgan."

Arthur could not believe what he was hearing. "How could my sister be involved in magic?"

"She turned out to be a black sorcerer, a person who uses magic for their own personal gain."

Arthur said, "I would like to have a minute on my own."

The royal guard kept an eye on him. Ten minutes later, a messenger came riding into the camp. The guards held him back.

He shouted, "I have a message for the King".

Arthur heard the shouting and said, "Let him into the camp."

The messenger spoke. "Morgan has an army and it's preparing to cross the border."

Arthur called a meeting with his Knights, Sir Gawain, Sir Ector and Sir Lancelot.

"You shall ride in front one day. Thank you Arthur. Your job will be to scout in front of the army to make sure that we do not get ambushed."

TR Eden

As they had a day in camp, Arthur called Merlin over and said that he trusted him as a friend to only use his powers to protect Camelot, and never to use them for himself.

Merlin got down on one knee and said, "God save the King."

Arthur smiled and told his friend to rise.

Merlin told the students to march behind the main guard. It was the safest place in the column.

Max was scared stiff. He kept on checking his shoe laces. He did not want to go into battle. Alison was so anxious her legs felt like they were made of lead. Knowing that they were heading for battle did not help with Jack's visions of images of death.

Mr Underwood could see the students shaking, so he took them to one side and said, "We need your help to get the shield for Devena."

The party reached the border between Morgan and Arthurs's kingdoms. They were shocked by what they saw. Morgan's army were camping 3 miles away from the border.

Arthur called a meeting between Merlin and his trusted Knights to try and come up with a plan of attack. Sir Lancelot advised caution. If Merlin was right and Morgan did posses magical abilities, she would be an extremely difficult opponent to beat.

"And there is another problem," he pointed out to Arthur, "She is still your half-sister and has a right to the throne of Camelot, as well as the Other-land."

Sir Ector had another idea, which was simply to build a wall between the two kingdoms. Arthur pointed out that that would take too long to do. The students asked if they could have a chat with Merlin for a few minutes. Merlin made his excuses to Arthur, saying that he wanted to chat to Princess Jade and her party.

Alternative Dimension 2

Mr Underwood asked, "Why don't you just invade? After all, Arthur does have a right to that kingdom and land."

Merlin replied, "The people of the Other-land have been an independent state for over 500 years. They had their own cultures and beliefs and they would cause a civil war if they thought their way of life was under threat."

Mr Underwood pointed out that Morgan was Arthur's half-sister, so how could she rule an independent country?

Merlin said, "It's because she has been educated to respect the traditions of the Other-land and not interfere with them. She was born and brought up to rule the Other-land, like Arthur has been brought up to rule Camelot."

The next morning the army was woken up by the sound of screaming. It was a sound that unnerved Max, Jack and Alison. Mr Underwood told his students to stay down. Merlin ordered the army to form a circle around the camp to protect Princess Jade, Arthur and their courts. Arrows were flying from all sides. Then Merlin noticed someone he knew. It was Brittany (long blonde hair, brown eyes, 5ft 6, dressed in her captain's uniform).

Merlin knew she was an incredible leader, but wondered why someone with her skills would be involved in a minor border infringement? In fact, she had been given secret orders from Morgan and was carrying them out.

Arthur needed to know what his half-sister was planning, so he sent three of his best Knights to capture a Sergeant from the attacking force, in order to question them on what Morgan was going to do that night.

Sir Ector, Sir Galahad and Sir Gawain rode across the border. They pretended to be a spy envoy, taking plans of Camelot back to Queen Morgan. They were stopped at the border, where they were asked to produce their order documents. There was a group of 20 solders at the border. Merlin had produced some fake orders to get them across the border.

TR Eden

The head guard (short black hair, blue eyes, 5ft 10, wore the uniform of a Morgan soldier), looked at the passes and allowed them to enter Morgan's Kingdom.

Sir Galahad, Sir Ector and Sir Gawain approached the camp. It was getting dark and they were really hungry, so they showed the Sergeant (dirty-brown hair, blue eyes and tatty uniform showing Morgan's coat of arms in the middle) who was second in charge of the camp their faked orders. After examining them, he ordered that they should have food and shelter.

Early the next morning, whilst most of the camp was asleep, they rushed over to the Sergeant's tent, grabbed him, tied him up and gagged him, then shoved him into an old wagon which was behind the tent. They placed a lot for straw on top of him, and then they headed back to the border. They told the guard they were going back to spy on King Arthur, and the old wagon was part of their disguise, as they were pretending to be farmers.

When they got back to camp, Merlin and Arthur questioned the Sergeant for information. He claimed to know nothing about Queen Morgan's intentions, he was just told to protect the camp. Merlin and Arthur saw that he was telling the truth. What they did not realise was that Morgan was performing a piece of relay magic, so she could see what the Sergeant could see. She saw Merlin's face and spat. She had no time for her former tutor! She then burst out laughing to herself. She had no intention of invading Camelot and fighting Arthur's supporters. She had something else in mind.

Alternative Dimension 2

Morgan's Knight

Morgan knew she would have to find a way to spy and interact with Arthur whilst he was in Camelot, without him noticing. She spent days going through her sorcery books to find something of use that would give her the upper hand. Although sorcerers did not use spells, they would quite often have a magic library for ideas on words, and plans of attack to use when casting sorcery.

Morgan had a massive library. Most of the books had been given to her by magic tribes who wanted her to take the throne of Camelot, so that she could restore the rights to perform magic freely. She spent days looking through her book collection without any luck. Then, all of a sudden, she came across a book covered in dust and spider's webs and with a broken spine. The book was entitled 'The Evil Lord's Encyclopaedia of Sorcery'. This book was pure black magic. The first page was blank. Then, all of a sudden, the book spoke.

"Only an evil sorcerer who believes in black magic can read this book."

A bolt of yellow light shot out and hit Morgan on the head. The book scanned her brain then, 5 seconds later, it said, "entry approved."

The plans of attack appeared in front of her. She looked through the book and reached a section called 'Control'. She started to smile. It was the same magic the Evil Lord used to control his subjects – where they operate as part of his mind, meaning the person is effectively dead because they would have no free will.

Morgan's magic was not as strong as the Evil Lords. But, as she read the book on how much energy it would take to control one person, she realised that was possible. So she used a communication stone to contact Brittany, and ordered her back to the castle straight away so that she could help her carry out the plan.

TR Eden

She told Brittany all about the plan to control one person and use them to spy on Arthur. Brittany was horrified. The idea of taking control of someone was too dark an idea for her, so she refused to help. Morgan made her a counter offer – she would agree or she would be turned into a toad.

When Brittany got back to the castle (which had taken her two days to ride across the Other-land), she entered the castle courtyard and headed for the Royal apartments where Morgan lived. She asked if she could have a session with Queen Morgan. Morgan agreed to meet her in the gallery.

As soon as Morgan entered the room, Brittany got down on one knee and said, "I am yours to command."

"That's better," Morgan said. She then smiled and told her friend to rise.

Brittany knew if the public heard that Morgan was going to use black magic against Arthur, then support for her would fall away. After all, he was very popular in both Kingdoms.

She voiced this to Morgan who replied, "They had better not find out."

Then she ordered Brittany to find a suitable person to use. So she went all over the castle trying to find people who would be easy to control. Morgan had told her that the person needed to be clever and strong.

In the courtyard Brittany lined up a hundred servants who might be of use. Morgan and Brittany interviewed them. They got their choice down to 20 people. The final selection was decided by tests. The first was an IQ test to find out if they were intelligent enough to communicate telepathically. The second test was to see how easy it was to communicate with them telepathically using Morgan's powers. The final test was horse-riding around the grounds, to see who had the best ability.

The following morning, Morgan announced to the court that she had her three finalists. They were Christopher (6ft 3,

Alternative Dimension 2

short brown hair, blue eyes, wears a chef costume because he worked as a cook), Jessica (5ft 11 inches, long black hair, brown eyes, wears a dirty servant's uniform because she was a gardener), and finally there was Mathew (6 ft 2, short blond hair, green eyes, wears costumes because he is a Court entertainer).

After probing their minds, Morgan decided to use Christopher for the experiment. He needed to be trained for his new role as a Knight of Camelot. Although Morgan would be controlling him, he still needed to develop his skills, especially combat.

Brittany started by teaching him sword skills. These lessons were incredibly important because he would have to learn how to defend the King. Brittany knew the secret to fighting was to get angry at the person you were attacking, so she started to point and laugh at him. This made him angry and he attacked Brittany with the full strength of his anger.

Morgan was watching from the window in the Great Hall. She was incredibly impressed by the speed he was showing in learning new skills.

Meanwhile, back at the battle on the border, Morgan had ordered her troops to pressure Arthur, so that he would have to go and find help from neighbouring Kingdoms. Arthur ordered Merlin to come and talk about battle tactics.

"We need more support if we are going to defeat Morgan's army," Arthur said, "especially if she decides to use black magic against us."

Merlin pointed out that his powers were more than a match for Morgan. But he agreed with Arthur. The more support they could get, the better their chance of victory.

So he said, "The nearest Kingdom is Borrek. It's a two-day ride away."

Uther had signed a treaty of mutual protection with this Kingdom.

TR Eden

Arthur asked Merlin, "Who should I send?"

Merlin suggested, "How about Princess Jade's Court?"

Arthur thought his old friend was mad to come up with a plan where the whole fate of the Kingdom lay in the hands of strangers, and he voiced his concerns to Merlin.

Merlin replied by saying, "There is no-one else to send. Everyone else is fighting in the battle over the border."

Arthur reluctantly agreed.

Merlin told the plan to Mr Underwood, who agreed it with the students, except for Max Jack and Alison. Max was pacing up-and-down, and Alison was so anxious she could not speak from her anxiety. The thought of the mission filled them with dread. All Jack could see were people in pain.

Back in the Other-land, Christopher's training had come to an end, so Morgan asked for him to be brought before her. She told him to hold her hand. As he did this, the control magic took effect. She smiled.

"Your new name is Emtoro."

Morgan used really dark black magic. She then used a lot of magical energy to transport him to the village the students were heading for. Morgan knew Arthur would go to Borrek, as it was the nearest Kingdom Camelot had a treaty with. She also understood Arthur. After all, she was his half-sister.

The school party had reached a forest, so they performed a communication spell on a translator rock. They wanted Merlin to help find them a safe route through the woodland. They could hear wild beasts that sounded like they were massive.

Merlin told them, "The best route is the quickest, so you are safer if you walk in a straight line. Those beasts you can hear are magical creatures. Uther had them banished from

Alternative Dimension 2

the farms and castle of Camelot. Like the centurions, half-man half-horse, they are about 7foot tall."

When they were 30 minutes into the forest, the party heard a galloping sound. Approaching them was the lead centurion and his guard. The group got down on one knee as a sign of respect. Mr Underwood explained that they needed to cross the forest to get support for Arthur's army.

The leading centurion spat. "Why should I help you, after Arthur's father hunted us down to near extinction?"

The students and Mr Underwood showed him their wands. He saw that they had magical abilities, and agreed to help them. He assumed they would treat enchanted creatures fairly. He agreed to escort them across his Kingdom, making sure they did not see any of their defences.

TR Eden

Morgan's Plan

The party finally reached their destination. Sir Emtoro was staying in the local pub called 'The Uther Arms'. When the group arrived, they went in search of the leader of the town's guards. A Captain (long blond hair, blue eyes, 5ft 11, wearing a gold uniform) saw them and went over to greet them.

Mr Underwood explained why they had come.

"Camelot is under attack from the Other-land," he said.

The Captain looked confused. Why would Arthur's sister be attacking her own brother's Kingdom?

Mr Underwood continued to explain.

"Morgan has become power-mad. She has a claim to the Kingdom, being Arthur's half-sister, and a lot of supporters within Camelot."

The Captain said that he would love to help, but that his troops had gone on a secret mission, and anyone who could fight had gone with them.

"Is their no-one who could help us?" Jade asked in a scared voice.

The Captain clicked his fingers.

"There is one Knight who arrived here looking for employment. Apparently his sword skills are legendary."

"Where is this person staying?" Mr Underwood asked.

The Captain smiled. "He is staying in 'The Uther Arms'."

After searching the town for the inn, they eventually found it in a small side street. It had a cobbled floor and large wooden buildings, with their tops over-hanging the street. When they knocked on the inn door, a small man (short

Alternative Dimension 2

black hair, brown eyes, 4ft 11, wore a dark black shirt with black trousers) appeared on the doorstep. He asked how he could help them.

Mr Underwood explained that they were looking for a talented, unemployed Knight. The inn keeper searched through his records, and found the number of the room Sir Emtoro was staying in. They went up a crooked set of stairs and found his room. They knocked on his bedroom door. Max wanted to check that the front door was shut. Alison was panicking about what could be on the other side of the door. Jack kept on visualising that they were about to be attacked by the Knight.

Slowly the door crept open.

The man inside asked, "How may I help you?"

It was Morgan, speaking through her controlled knight like a ventriloquist's dummy.

Mr Underwood explained about attacks from the Other-land, and the fact that Arthur needed all the help he could get to defend the border. Mr Underwood pointed out that, if he helped to protect Camelot, he may find employment as Knight of Camelot. He agreed straight away, or rather Morgan did.

They had to travel back through the enchanted forest.

Jade shouted out, "This is the Princess that you helped earlier. We need an escort back through your forest for our safety."

The unicorns had hearing 100 times better than a human, so two centurions arrived to escort them safely back through the forest. When they got back to Arthur, Sir Emtoro got down on one knee and begged for the chance to prove himself worthy of becoming one of his Knights.

Arthur said, "Very well, you can take control of the Royal Guard and force back Morgan's army."

TR Eden

So Sir Emtoro organised a charge straight at Morgan's army, which just ran away. Of course Morgan had rigged this to gain Arthur's trust for her new Knight. Arthur congratulated his troops and Knights, but he mainly praised Sir Emtoro for scaring Morgan's army back into the Other-land.

Merlin remained unconvinced, thinking that it was too easy that the army had just run away, rather than continuing to fight. But everything had gone as Morgan had planned, and she now had a spy in Camelot.

Alternative Dimension 2

Arthur Accepts the Knight

On the way back to Camelot, Arthur talked to Merlin about the new Knight who led the attack. He was extremely pleased with the amount of bravery he had shown. Merlin could sense something was terribly wrong, so he urged Arthur to be cautious. He knew that he could not talk to Arthur about his true feelings, because Arthur was the King after all, and Merlin had sworn an oath to stand by him as a leader.

He did, however, speak to Mr Underwood.

"Don't you find it odd that the army ran as soon as they saw the advance? They did not even try to defend themselves. I don't trust the new Knight Sir Emtoro. I sense that he is somehow acting under Morgan's influence."

Merlin realised he could feel a magical force around him, like strong black magic.

"I think he is mentally linked to Morgan," he said.

Mr Underwood asked Merlin, "What's the next move?"

Merlin pointed out that they would have to be cautious.

"If Arthur knew we were plotting against one of his favourites, he would have our heads for treason."

Meanwhile, in the Great Hall, Arthur was introducing Sir Emtoro to his Court and his Knights. Arthur took him to one side, and explained that his Knights were guardians of peace and law throughout his Kingdom. He praised Sir Emtoro.

"You showed great courage in your attack on the Other-land. Would you like to join my Knights of Camelot?"

Morgan spoke through Sir Emtoro and replied, "I would be grateful for the opportunity to serve your Kingdom."

TR Eden

"Very well," Arthur said, "repeat after me. I swear my allegiance to you and the Kingdoms of Camelot and the Other-land."

When Arthur told Merlin that he intended to make Sir Emtoro a Knight of Camelot, Merlin became increasingly worried, although he did not let Arthur see his concerns.

The next day, Arthur put Sir Emtoro through the rituals of Camelot. The first ritual was to lift an object of the Kings choosing. Arthur chose a pile of stones which were about as heavy as a small car. Sir Emtoro could not lift it. Morgan, refusing to be out done, performed levitation magic. She got Sir Emtoro to touch the stone so that it looked like he was lifting it.

The next ritual was a race against a giant sea serpent, around an island in a massive lake. This lake does not exist in our dimension. This ritual had been banned under Uther because he hated magical creatures.

Merlin asked the sea serpent if he was ready to start. He nodded. Merlin then asked Sir Emtoro if he was ready. He stuck a thumb up.

Merlin created a large explosive noise, and the race began. As soon as Sir Emtoro hit the water, Morgan turned him into a half-fish creature. The magic lasted 20 minutes, which was just enough time for him to win the race.

The final challenge was a sword fight. This filled Morgan with dread. She would be unable to help Sir Emtoro because she could not cast her magic fast enough to be used in a fight. The person Sir Emtoro would be fighting was Sir Lancelot.

The battle began, and Lancelot was soon winning. He eventually knocked the sword out of Sir Emtoro's hand.

Arthur addressed Sir Emtoro and asked him to get down on one knee.

Alternative Dimension 2

"You have courage, skills and honour," he said, "I hereby make you a Knight of Camelot."

The students, Mr Underwood and Merlin realised things had just become more complicated.

TR Eden

Merlin Meets the Chosen Ones

Mr Underwood took Merlin to one side and suggested that he should meet the chosen ones. Merlin thought about it for a minute, and then said he would.

"However Arthur will not approve me leaving during a national emergency," he said.

Mr Underwood pointed out, "You will have to come alone. We cannot allow non-magical people to see our fake island."

So Merlin met with Arthur, and said, "Princess Jade wants to go back to her Kingdom. But it will mean crossing three other friendly Kingdoms between here and the sea."

Arthur said the party would need an escort, and suggested, "Why don't you take some of my private guard to defend you?"

Merlin knew this wouldn't work for two reasons: one, no outsiders could set foot on their island and two, the chosen ones would not trust the guard, given how Uther had hunted down people who possessed magic.

So he made up an excuse saying, "We are going to travel disguised as villagers, taking crops of apples down to the port to trade. So if we show any sign of force our cover will be broken."

Arthur agreed, thinking that a show of force could slow them down crossing the borders.

The party left that morning. As they marched off, Max, Jack and Alison were feeling a lot better, knowing they were going back to the safety of their island. It was a long journey after travelling for a couple of days as they had.

Mr Underwood asked Merlin, "Surely we can use transport magic?"

Alternative Dimension 2

Merlin replied, "Because I do not know the exact location of the island, if I get my calculations wrong and we reappear in the wrong Kingdom, we may end up in a Kingdom that does not trust magic. But we can use it to get back, because we will go back the same way we came."

The group finally reached the coast. The water was a bit choppy so Mr Underwood doubted that they would be able to cross it. Merlin smiled and performed levitation magic.

At first it looked like it had not made a difference. Then Merlin stepped on to the water and he was floating above it.

When they arrived at the island, Merlin was amazed by what he saw. Whilst walking around the village, Abby sensed Merlin's presence and went out to meet him. She advised him to see Pedro the wand-maker. Merlin had never felt this accepted in his whole life. As he walked off to Pedro's shop, he couldn't believe how many different sorts of people there were. Some with two heads, or heads inside their stomachs. Even Merlin found the place totally overwhelming.

The students escorted Merlin to Pedro the wand-maker (has two mouths, one on his head and one in his stomach, green bone palate, like a stegosaurs, cat-like ears, purple eyes, body made up with orange fur).

When they arrived there, Pedro went into shock.

"You're Mer...mer...merlin!" he said.

Merlin smiled, "That's right. I was told you could make a wand that is totally unique to me."

Pedro smiled from both sets of mouths, and said it would be an honour. So he used some of his best quality absorbing wood, and bonded it to Merlin's DNA by getting him to hold it.

When Merlin left the shop, there was a huge crowd cheering and applauding. Everyone wanted to shake his hand. He was saved from the mob by two teachers, Mr Martin (looked like a cat, long pointed orange ears, blue eyes, whiskers, about 30cm long, his body was covered in ornate fur), and Mr Fletcher (blond hair, red eyes, orange skin on the face and blond fur). They performed a force-field spell, so that no-one could get near.

Merlin was a bit upset. He was enjoying the fact that, for once, he was being accepted. They escorted Merlin to the chosen ones' area. They reached a small room where they all sat down for a chat.

"Why did you invite me here?" Merlin asked.

Abby explained, "We need the shield. It could help stop the most evil force in any dimension. Devena, the witch Queen needs the shield to help in the fight against him."

Ralph clicked his fingers. "Would you feel happier if you were to meet Devena?"

He nodded, so Abby used her crystal ball to contact her, repeating the word 'shield' over and over again. Devena appeared straight away.

She asked Merlin "Would it make you feel better if we perform a truth scan?"
He agreed straight away. A truth scan was basically a lie detector that could be performed by two magical beings. Merlin and Devena closed their eyes and opened their minds. Merlin and Devena were both touching the crystal ball to get a strong link. Merlin probed deep into Devena's mind which caused her to scream out in pain. He could see how intelligent she was and how she respected all types of life, so he came to the conclusion that she would never use the shield for evil.

Mr Underwood pointed out that they had better head back to Camelot. The group had completely lost track of time. Jade had been invited to a private party.

Merlin was about to perform the transport spell when, all of a sudden, Mr Shaw took the students into his office, saying that he understood that the three of them were scared. He told them he could not force them to go, but pointed out the two reasons why they should go. The first was that they had a lot of magical potential, and any extra magical energy may help on the mission. The second was that this was their world in another dimension, so they know more about it than anyone else.

In the school, Max started pacing up-and-down, thinking he had forgotten something. Alison was so anxious she was shaking from fright, and Jack's images were getting worse. Max said he did not feel up to it.

Mr Shaw replied, "Sometimes we have to face our fears to allow us to complete our goals in life."

The three of them thought about it, and then agreed to go on the mission to Camelot.

TR Eden

Improving Morale

When they got back to the castle, Merlin welcomed Jade and her court to the banquet. It was there he told her about the history of the island. Max, Jack and Alison paid attention to the lecture. They were keen to see how different the two dimensions were.

"The vast island is divided up into 25 Kingdoms and tribal land. This is land that, by tradition, belongs to the King, but was handed over so the people could be independent and make up their own rules on how it should be governed. Like the witch tribes that Uther banished whilst he was King, and several independent villages, most of them are friendly and trade with Camelot. But because of its wealth and code of honour, Camelot is seen as the central trading place for the island."

Mr Underwood asked Arthur, "How is the castle one of the oldest forts that we have come across?"

Arthur smiled and asked if the visitors would like to hear the legend about the creation of Camelot? They all nodded.

Arthur said, "Very well. The legend begins in the dark time. There was a lot of fighting and violence between the villages. Then one day a man came up with a peaceful solution, to merge the villages into one Kingdom, allowing more farmers to work on the land rather than fighting each other.

"But the Kingdom became too big for one person, so it was split into Camelot and the Other-land. The first in-line to Camelot would be the first born from the founder of the peace agreement. The Other-land would be run by the second in-line. Of course, this happened over 500 years ago and there are no records left to prove that this is exactly what happened."

That evening, Jade was sitting on the top table with Arthur. The Knights,

Alternative Dimension 2

Nobles and Jade's court sat on the second table, slightly lower down than the first. The rest of the court sat on the lowest tables.

When a security meeting is called, the knights and the King sit at the round table, because each of their viewpoints is as important as the Kings. When it came to banquets, the court was more formally arranged to keep discipline, and allow the court to see their King at the top or highest point.

Arthur started to talk about the tremendous burden of running a Kingdom, and he wondered how Jade coped. Jade froze. She could not think of an answer. Then Mr Underwood asked if he could answer on Jade's behalf.

"Although she is young," Mr Underwood said, "Jade believes that the main role of a leader is to listen to their subjects' advice, and, when appropriate, act on it."

Arthur called out "Send for the horse master," (black hair, blue eyes, about 5ft10, wearing the robes of office), "I wish to ride tomorrow to the horse master."

Arthur smiled, "A tour around my Kingdom will allow the subjects a chance to see the King."

Arthur especially wanted to visit the four command posts on the front-line. If ever there were an invasion, the troops manning the position would light a bonfire if they saw any sign of an invasion whilst on tour. Merlin knew he would have to tell Arthur the whole story, but did not know where to begin.

Arthur saw his friend looking worried, so he gave him a pat on the back and said, "You can tell me anything."

Merlin started from the beginning.

"You know the legend of the shield? Well, it's all true."

Arthur looked shocked. "How was it created?" he asked.

TR Eden

Merlin continued to explain about the fact that his half-sister was an exceptional sorcerer.

"I thought I could teach her the good in magic" Merlin said, "But she saw how she could use it for herself to gain total power. She followed all of my teachings. However, 5 years later, she turned to black magic."

Merlin explained the difference between white magic and black magic. He then told Arthur about the shield, and the fact that they could not collect it until they knew Morgan could not get it herself.

Arthur called his Knights to plan an attack on the Other-land and capture Morgan.

Unfortunately for them, Morgan heard everything through Sir Emtoro, so she knew they were going to attack, and was able to prepare for it.

Alternative Dimension 2

The Battle

When they reached the border, Arthur ordered his Knights into his command tent to talk about the upcoming battle.

Sir Gawain began by saying, "I will command the entire attack."

Arthur shook his head, and said "Gawain, you have served me and my father with dedication and honesty, I need you here to help protect the camp."

Merlin, who did not trust Sir Emtoro, suggested, "Why doesn't Sir Emtoro go on the mission?"

This filled Morgan with dread. If Sir Emtoro left the camp, she would not be able to see what was going on.

Arthur thought about it, and then agreed. He pointed out, however, that he would feel more comfortable if an experienced knight went with him and the troops. So Arthur picked Sir Ector to go with him. He suggested that they should march at midnight for a night attack. It would take them by surprise.

Morgan was in her castle smiling to herself. She knew exactly what they were planning, so she sent her entire force to meet them head on. Morgan knew she had to be careful, as some of her army were loyal to Arthur. After all, technically it was his kingdom. Most people in the Other-land, however, preferred being semi-independent from Camelot.

The battle between Brittany's army against Sir Ector and Sir Emtoro was extremely tense. Morgan could see every move they were making, as Brittany used a communication stone to talk to Morgan. Seeing that Arthur was not fighting confused Morgan. Arthur usually led from the front. He was up to something, but she had no way of telling what.

Merlin and Arthur told the remaining group of people that the battle was a diversion, to allow the remainder of the trusted knights, and Princess Jade's court, to cross the border. Whilst Morgan was distracted, she would be totally defenceless.

Using her communication stone, Brittany expressed some concerns to Morgan. Now that Sir Emtoro was not in Arthur's company, she no longer had a way of monitoring his movements. She also expressed concerns that this could be a diversion tactic, to take Morgan and the castle by surprise.

Morgan said, "Don't worry, I have a plan."

She went into her back garden, where there was a graveyard dedicated to the most powerful knights that had ever existed. Strangely though, they were arranged in a star-like pattern. In the centre, there was a star painted on the floor.

Morgan walked over, stood in the star and cried out, "Arise." The coffins all flung open and the skeletons got down on one knee. The leader of the Other-land assumed command. She ordered the skeleton army not to allow anyone access to her castle.

As King Arthur's diversionary party marched on the Other-land, they noticed that there was not one single guard on patrol, which Merlin found very odd.

He pointed out to Arthur, "You would think she would have left some sort of guard to stop us sneaking into the kingdom."

Arthur thought his friend was over-reacting, and said, "Our plan has worked perfectly! She was totally distracted by the battle."

Merlin still thought she was up to something. When they got to the castle, they saw the skeleton knights, and noticed that they surrounded the whole building. Merlin was impressed by the amount of magical energy it must have taken to raise the dead.

Alternative Dimension 2

Arthur smiled, "This should be easy, four to one."

Merlin pointed out, "If those skeletons are powered by magical energy, this could be harder than you think."

He advised Mr Underwood and the students, "Whatever happens, don't let Morgan know you have magical powers, otherwise you will become targets as well."

Mr Underwood asked, "What if she senses magic in us like you did?"

Merlin responded, "Her powers are not as strong at detecting magical disturbances as mine."

Most of the students felt slightly worried about the oncoming attack, but knew they were relatively safe with Merlin around. All except Max, Jack and Alison. Max was pacing up-and-down, trying to remember if he had forgotten anything. He always marched in a straight line backwards and forwards. Alison could hardly speak, and Jack kept on visualising all of them dying as they were killed by the skeleton knights.

Mr Underwood said he would protect them and make sure they would be safe, but this did not reassure them because of what had happened in Antarctica.

TR Eden

The Skeleton War

Arthur launched a full-scale attack on the skeletons, but their weapons were useless. Every time one of them was defeated, they would put their heads, arms or legs back on and continue fighting.

Merlin could sense something wrong, and believed Morgan had known they were coming. He thought there must be a spy in Camelot that had informed her about the plan to split forces. Morgan would also know they would come for her, which gave her time to prepare for their arrival. He voiced his concerns to Arthur, who pointed out that all of his army was absolutely trustworthy.

Merlin, however, knew that Morgan had to have been thinking about it for at least 5 hours in order to generate enough magical energy to raise the dead.

The battle began. Arthur thought that it would be easy to destroy the skeleton army. After all, they were not wearing armour, nor had any shields to protect themselves. Arthur led the attack by attacking the person he thought was the leader, and chopped his head off. The skeleton just bent down, picked up his head and started to fight again. It soon dawned on Merlin that, if the skeletons kept on picking themselves up after every attack, they would eventually tire out his troops. After all, skeletons did not get tired, nor do they need a break to rest.

Merlin realised that their only hope was a diversion, so that Morgan's concentration would be broken. Merlin turned to the students and smiled.

"All of you posses magical powers. Morgan will be able to sense something different about you."

Mr Underwood was alarmed. "What if she realises we are wizards? That could be a direct threat to her and her Kingdom."

Alternative Dimension 2

Merlin pointed out, "Her sense about magic is not as strong as mine. She will sense something about you, but will not realise what it is."

Mr Underwood still had doubts. "If you are wrong, then the students' lives will be in danger."

Merlin said, "We have no choice, we have to try."

The students were scared, especially Max, Jack and Alison. They kept on thinking about the time they went into the temple in Antarctica, and were petrified that their new friends might also die. They went to Mr Underwood and explained their fears.

Mr Underwood appreciated how they felt, but he needed them and their knowledge of Morgan.

"After all, it might be a different dimension, but this is still Earth and you know more about it than the rest of us."

They thought about it, and then agreed to help. They walked up to the gate.

While Arthur and his men continued fighting the skeleton army, Mr Underwood knocked on a door that was next to the gate.

Morgan looked into her crystal ball to see who it was. She saw it was a bunch of children. She sensed something unusual about them, so she let them into the castle. Her servants escorted them to the throne room, where Mr Underwood spoke.

"I wish to present our Princess."

Jade stepped forward. "I am a Princess from a far-away land, who has come to pay tribute to you."

"Are you involved with my brother outside?" Morgan asked, "You turned up just as he started attacking my castle?"

"No, we are neutral in this conflict. We only travelled with Arthur for protection," Jade replied.

Morgan still had a strange feeling about them, so she looked Mr Underwood straight in the eye and asked him, "Why have you come here?"

Mr Underwood did not answer. A few seconds later he asked about the shield of Excalibur. Morgan gritted her teeth.

"That's a secret between me and Merlin. If you know of this, Merlin must trust you. I do not trust anyone connected to Merlin."

She yelled to her guards to hold them and throw them into the dungeon, until she decided what to do with them. Whilst she was distracted, thinking how much she hated Merlin for telling outsiders about the shield, her concentration broke and the skeletons fell to the floor.

Alternative Dimension 2

Arthur's invasion

The attacking party, led by Arthur, burst into Morgan's throne room. She smiled.

"Welcome brother", she said.

The two had a long chat about their past, growing up in Camelot. Arthur also told Morgan about the night their father died, saying he loved them both very much.
Morgan spat. She hated the way that he thought all magic was evil and punished anyone who used it.

Merlin then entered the room. He tasked Morgan to speak in the old tongue. This was the language of powerful sorcerers. Merlin smiled.

"You have come a long way since the lessons I taught you in secret. Why did you decide to use black magic just to benefit yourself, rather than helping others?"

Morgan replied, "For over 30 years you kept your powers secret from King Uther and those other sceptics. The only reason they like you is because you conform to their way of life. You are not allowed to show your true self to them. If you used your powers you could overthrow Arthur and take the kingdom for yourself."

Merlin replied, "If I did that I would lose myself. I would become obsessed with power and just think of myself."

Morgan smiled. "I have everything I could ever want by using my powers to create it for me."

Merlin said in normal speech, "You have my friends. I want them released. I challenge you to a sorcery duel."

Meanwhile, in the prison, the students were becoming worried and upset, not just Max, Jack and Alison.

Back in the throne room, Arthur asked Merlin, "What is a sorcery duel?"

TR Eden

Merlin explained, "It's an ancient tradition. Whoever wins gets control of the other person. So if I win, Morgan will be forced to release the prisoners. If she wins, I will have to do everything she says."

Arthur pointed out that it was too risky. "If she gains control of you we would have no defence against your combined powers."

Merlin then said, "I have to protect Jade and her court. Don't ask me why. If Morgan becomes too powerful she will learn the ultimate black magic spell, the one for eternal life, and rule forever."

Alternative Dimension 2

Sorcery Duel

Merlin walked back to Morgan and said he was ready to begin. Merlin reached into his pocket to grab something. It was a coin, which he gave to Arthur.

"What do I do with this?" he asked Merlin.

Merlin replied, "We are going to decide who goes first."

Morgan called tails, leaving Merlin with heads.

"Ready?" Morgan asked.

Merlin smiled, "More than ready."

Arthur threw the coin in the air. It landed on tails. Morgan chose the first challenge, a sword fight. But these were not just any swords, they were enchanted swords.

Arthur asked, "What is an enchanted sword?"

Merlin explained, "An enchanted sword absorbs the magical energy of the person using it. The more powerful you are, the more powerful your sword will become."

They were ready to begin. Morgan was allowed the first attack, which meant Merlin was defending. As her sword struck his, Merlin was amazed at how powerful it was.

Arthur asked, "What do you have to do to win the battle?"

Merlin shouted out, "It's the first to draw blood."

It was time for Merlin to attack and Morgan to defend. Merlin used all of his strength in the attack to break Morgan's grip, but she was a lot younger than Merlin so she was able to repel the attack. Merlin then knew, given her magic ability and body strength, she would be impossible to beat in this challenge. When Morgan attacked for the second time, Merlin was already quite tired. He tried to hold on to his

sword and force back the attack, but he was too weak.
Morgan took the opportunity and cut his arm.

One of Morgan's servants shouted out, "That was incredible!"

Merlin conceded that he had lost the first task.

Next it was time for the second challenge, which was Merlin's choice. He chose a transformation duel. This meant that he could decide on a particular creature that they would use to fight each other.

Merlin chose dragons. Merlin turned into a cool blue dragon, while Morgan turned into a fiery red dragon. In this challenge, Merlin would have the upper hand, because it took a lot of magical energy to transform into something as big as a dragon.

At first it looked like the battle was going Morgan's way. She showed great speed in her attacks on Merlin, biting his tale several times. But after a while she started to slow down, because of the magical energy that it took to remain in dragon form. Merlin knew that if he hung on long enough, she would be unable to fight.

He was right. She became so tired that she stood in the centre of the room, trying to breath at a normal rate. When Merlin saw this he attacked as fast as possible. He blew a large fire ball which hit Morgan, and she turned back into human form.

Morgan looked at Merlin and said, "One match each. Now it's my turn for my last challenge."

Morgan's choice was a spell-casting contest. This meant attacking each other using wizard magic, which meant knowledge about spells.

Morgan said, "You know the rules. We stand back-to-back, walk forward ten spaces, turn around and then use your spell."

Alternative Dimension 2

Merlin hoped that the white magic attacker spell would be strong enough to knock Morgan out before she could use her magic. He cast the spell and bright yellow light shot from his wand. Then Morgan stuck out her hand and used a piece of magic Merlin did not know about. She held out her hand, closed her eyes and absorbed Merlin's magical energy. She then performed a divesting spell, using the combined magical energy of Merlin and herself. The amount of power that came out of the wand was enough to send Merlin flying backwards.

Merlin picked himself up and said, "It's my choice for the final challenge."

Merlin needed to come up with a challenge that relied on pure magical energy. He challenged Morgan to a race around a giant lake within the Other-land border.

"The rules are simple. You can turn into any creature, but you must stay as that creature for the whole race."

Merlin turned into a massive phoenix, whilst Morgan turned into a flying snake. They asked Arthur if he could start counting down from ten. When he reached zero the race would start.

Arthur started to count, "10, 9, 8, 7, 6, 5, 4, 3, 2, 1. Let the race begin."

They took off and started to travel at a speed of about ten miles an hour. Morgan got alongside Merlin and smiled. She had chosen a giant snake which had venom. She tried to bite the phoenix that was Merlin, but Merlin took evasive action.

When they reached the halfway-point they were neck-and-neck, but Morgan's concentration was starting to fade away. She started to slow down, and then stopped altogether. Merlin completed the course and won the challenge. The duel was a dead heat.

TR Eden

Arthur asked, "What happens next?"

Merlin explained, "If there is a dead heat we go to a sorcery duel."

"How does that work?" Arthur asked.

Merlin explained, "We each send a beam of magical energy from our wands. Whoever forces their opponent to drop their wand wins the tournament."

Morgan went up to Merlin and asked him if he was ready. Merlin smiled and said that he was born ready. Both sorcerers stood back-to-back, and then walked to the ends of the duelling zone, which was basically a straight piece of carpet. They had to stand on the edge of the carpet. Arthur was asked to count down to the start of the duel.

"10, 9, 8, 7, 6, 5, 4, 3, 2, 1"

Both sides sent out a beam of pure magic from their wands. The light was so bright it was like looking at the sun. The beam travelled backwards and forwards. Morgan was weakening, so Merlin used all his magical strength for one minute, and increased the intensity of his beam. Morgan's wand was starting to become hot. She tried to hold on to it but, in the end, she dropped it.

She picked it up, gave it to Merlin and said, "My life is at your command."

Alternative Dimension 2

Morgan's imprisonment

Whilst being escorted from her castle, Morgan noticed something strange in Sam's pocket. It was the top of his wand, which was poking out. Morgan suddenly realised, the reason she had a feeling about them was because they possessed magic.

That night they made camp, and Arthur told Merlin that he now had a big problem. He had captured Morgan.

"Where shall we imprison her? We can't take her back to Camelot."

Being Arthur's half-sister meant that there was an underground movement to replace Arthur with Morgan. These were mainly people who wanted to be able to practice magic anywhere. These people did not trust Arthur, given how his father treated people with magic. They preferred Morgan, because they had heard that she possessed magic. So Arthur asked Merlin for any suggestions.

Merlin pretended to think for five minutes on the problem, but he knew the answer straight away.

He suggested, "Morgan should be imprisoned in Princess Jade's kingdom. After all, it is an island that would be easy to defend."

Arthur thought about it, and then agreed. It was the best way forward.

Mr Underwood took Merlin to one side, and asked "What if her troops try to recapture her from our island?"

Merlin told them to relax. They would have to march through Camelot and several other kingdoms to reach the coast. Merlin knew that Arthur could not see the population of the island, as the people who lived there were in their true form from other dimensions. He told Arthur that Princess Jade and her court would have to transport Morgan without using any of Arthur's troops.

TR Eden

Arthur asked Merlin how he thought that he would be able to hold Morgan captive.

Merlin said, "Because her life now belongs to me, and all sorceresses own the sorceresses' code."

So Arthur agreed to split forces and allow Jade's court to escort Morgan to their island.

That night, around the campfire, Morgan asked Merlin how long he had known that these people possessed magic, telling him that she had seen a wand poking out of one of their pockets.

Merlin came clean. He explained that Morgan would be imprisoned on a magical island full of wizards.

"It is the only place that will be able to contain you and your powers."

Merlin and Morgan spent the rest of the evening talking over old times. Merlin then asked her straight out whether she would be willing to use her powers to help people, and not just herself.

Morgan turned around and looked at Merlin straight in the eye.

She said, "I have become powerful using my magic for myself, and I like getting everything that I want."

The next day the group discovered a deserted piece of land. Merlin smiled.

"This is exactly what I have been looking for."

"Why do you want an empty area of land?" Mr Underwood asked.

Merlin pointed out that, because Morgan was such a dangerous prisoner, he wanted to complete the last part of the trip using transport magic. And given the amount of

Alternative Dimension 2

energy it would take, people would be able to see them transport.

Max said that he did not want to go. He hated transport magic at the best of times, but on this scale he was scared that it would go wrong and that they would not make their destination. He was so upset that he started pacing up-and-down. Alison was so anxious she could not talk, and Jack's images were becoming incredibly violent.

Merlin took them to one side.

"It will be perfectly safe," he explained. "We can't take the risk of Morgan's enemies trying to rescue her."

Merlin performed the magic and the group were transported to the island.

When they got there, Morgan was escorted to the courtroom. Inside the court, Ralph read out the charges she was accused of; using black magic against her own subjects.

"How do you plead?" Ralph asked.

Morgan smiled. "Guilty."

Ralph gave his verdict.

"You will be imprisoned here until Arthur says you can be released."

Morgan smiled again. Her plan was coming together nicely.

Merlin breathed a sigh of relief. It meant that Arthur could collect the shield without interference.

TR Eden

The Journey to the Shield

Merlin told the selected students that they were going off to collect the shield, so he performed the transport magic again. They ended up in a clearing in the middle of a wood, about ten miles away from Camelot. Max was wondering whether he had forgotten something important, so he told Mr Underwood that he would like to go back to the island and try to remember what he had left behind.

Merlin turned round and gave him a hug, saying "I know you don't handle stress very well, but we have to get to the shield as soon as possible."

Jack's images were becoming incredibly bad, but he knew what would happen if the shield fell into the hands of the Evil Lord, so he forced himself to go on and find it.

Alison was so anxious her legs felt like lead-weights, every step felt like the gravity was twice as strong.

When they arrived back in Camelot, Merlin went to Arthur and said, "It's time for the quest."

"What quest?" Arthur asked.

"The one to collect the shield," Merlin replied.

"Well, where is it?"

Merlin finally revealed it was in the enchanted lake, and that it was being protected by the Lady-of-the-lake.

They would have to cross a barbarian kingdom to get there. These were not like barbarians from our dimension; they were people who believed in magic. Uther had called them barbarians because of their beliefs. They believed that magic was more powerful than science. They had all sworn an oath to kill Uther or any of his decedents, if they dared to enter their kingdom.

Alternative Dimension 2

Alison asked Merlin in a timid voice, "What did Uther do to them?"

Merlin explained, "When Uther was a young king, most of the realms of the island believed in magic in some form or another. But Uther started the crusades, believing that all magic would lead to black magic because of the temptation to use it to help you become powerful. So Uther created the neutral zone, an area that would be free from magic. The only problem was that this neutral zone infringed on several other kingdoms, meaning that Uther evicted people with magic from their homes.

Merlin had a word with Arthur in private.

"If you are serious about going on this journey, I suggest that you go in disguise. You will have to dress as a peasant. You will also have to leave your bodyguard behind."

Arthur was starting to worry. If he left his bodyguard behind, he would have no protection from the barbarians. Merlin pointed out that, if he marched with too many people, they might suspect who he was. Arthur reluctantly agreed, but insisted that Princess Jade and her court came on the journey.

Mr Underwood agreed on behalf of the students, but Max, Jack and Alison were petrified about what might happen to them when they entered the barbarians' kingdom.

The journey would take two days. Arthur had taken two of his knights for protection, Lancelot and Gawain.

That night they came to a village with an old tavern. It was full of dirt and rats, but it was the safest place to stay for the night.

The next day the tavern was surrounded by barbarian guards.

"How did they know who we are? We are in disguise!" Arthur said.

TR Eden

Merlin had an idea, but kept it to himself. There were two ways they might have known where they were: the first was that there could be a spy in Camelot, and the second was that they may have detected the magical energy coming from him and the students.

The barbarians outside were chanting, "We want Arthur! We want Arthur! Come out or we will attack the tavern using our powers!"

Arthur, Merlin, Lancelot and Gawain, plus Jade and her court came out. They were escorted to the barbarian magic Lord, who told Arthur that he had to answer for his father's crimes.

"But we will treat you fairly and put you on trial," the barbarian magic Lord said.

The courthouse was a massive stone circle. The witnesses were sitting in a theatre box. On the other side sat the judge, who read out the charges to Arthur.

"You are charged that, like your father, you intend to persecute us and force us to lose more territory. How do you plead?"

"Not guilty," Arthur said.

"Very well, let the trial begin."

Merlin interrupted, and said "Arthur is nothing like his father. He accepts me as both a sorcerer and his most trusted advisor."

"Can you prove this?" the judge asked.

Merlin stuck his hand in his pocket and pulled out his wand.

"Why else would he let me keep this, or even let me show it to you now? If I performed some magic, Arthur would not stop me."

Alternative Dimension 2

He pointed his wand at a massive mouse and shouted, "Transformo!" The mouse turned into a small cat.

The barbarian King accepted that Arthur did not have the same hatred for magic.

"Very well," he said, "you may pass through my kingdom."

Meanwhile, back in her prison cell, Morgan was watching the group's progress. What the party did not realise was that, whilst being escorted, she had placed an image stone in Sam's pocket so she was able to see what was going on as it transmitted. She had no idea where the group was heading.

The party walked for two hours through empty countryside until, eventually, they reached the lake. It looked beautiful. The water was crystal clear.

Arthur shouted out, "Enchanted Lady! We have travelled far to find you."

There was no response, so he tried again.

Merlin tapped Arthur on the shoulder. "The only person who can summon her is the magical doctor."

Merlin pointed out to Arthur that, if anyone could summon her, she would be inundated with requests.

"Where does he live?" Arthur enquired.

Merlin pointed to a small shack by the cliff edge, which was releasing smoke from the fire.

"What are we waiting for?" Arthur asked, "Let's go and get him."

Merlin shook his head, and said that he would have to go alone.

TR Eden

Merlin levitated to the top of the cliff. He knocked on the door. It creaked open, revealing a small man (brown hair, blue eyes, about 5ft, he was wearing the robes of the lake which was official uniform - they were pure gold). The man spoke.

"Hello old friend," he said, "What can I do to help?"

Merlin said, "I need to speak to the Lady-of-the-lake."

His friend replied, "I gathered that, but for what reason?"

Merlin pointed out that he was not going to like it.

"I want the shield of Excalibur," Merlin said.

The doctor looked at him.

"Are you sure? You know of its power. That's why you gave it to the lake in the first place."

Merlin smiled. "When I did that I only gave it to you because I thought this was the safest place. But I did not realise how powerful Morgan had become. If she keeps on learning at this rate, she will learn the magic of immortality. If she ever learned how to enslave the Lady-of-the-lake she would become the supreme ruler, not just of this kingdom but of the world."

The doctor asked Merlin if he knew of a safer place for the shield.

Merlin nodded. "Yes I do. It will be stored in Camelot under my guard."

"Very well," the doctor said, "I will go to the lake and summon the Lady first thing in the morning."

Meanwhile, the doctor was preparing some food for Merlin and the court. He apologised for the fact that Arthur's people would have to camp outside, as there was no space for them in his house.

Alternative Dimension 2

That night they had nettle soup, which was surprisingly tasty. Arthur organised a night-watch over the camp, then went to bed.

The following morning, the doctor woke them up and said that it was time they walked down to the edge of the lake.

The doctor stuck his magical wand into the water and said, "Arise!"

The centre of the lake started to bubble. Then a beautiful blonde woman with piercing green eyes appeared. She asked why she had been summoned.
The doctor explained that Merlin had come for the shield. She looked stunned. Merlin walked to the lake and got down on one knee. She smiled.

"Welcome old friend. Why do you want the shield?" she asked.

Merlin explained his reasons to her.

She responded, "There is another reason. I have seen a small bit of the future. The shield will be needed, but I can trust only you with it."

"Very well," Merlin said, "I will take it back to Camelot and encase it in stone. Only the true leader of Britain will be able to lift it."

The Lady agreed to Merlin's suggestion and released the shield.

The party made it back to Camelot without any problems. Word was obviously getting around about Arthur not being like his father, as he did not persecute people.

TR Eden

Morgan the Dragon Speaker

Now that she knew where the shield was, Morgan set about escaping her prison. On the magical island and the transformed ship, she had kept a dark secret about her powers. She was not just a sorcerer, but also a dragon-speaker, meaning that she could send telepathic messages to dragons and, hopefully, they would respond to her. She knew that, given the history between Camelot and the dragons, they would be more than willing to help her.

The dragons were a very powerful ancient society. They were also caring creatures. If one got into trouble, the other dragons would use telepathic skills to help that dragon.

So Morgan sent a message to their leader, the dragon Lord.

"Why should we help you?" he asked.

Morgan said, "I know how Uther organised a crusade to wipe you out, which failed. However he did successfully drive your people from their rightful kingdom. If you help me escape, I will use the combined forces of Camelot and the Other-land to help claim back your land."

The dragon Lord said he would think about it.

Meanwhile, Merlin and the students told Arthur they were going to collect some herbs.

Arthur smiled and said, "Of course. If Princess Jade wants to go with you she is more than welcome to do so."

They travelled for two miles through fields and woods, until they found a clearing suitable to perform transport magic. Merlin wanted to go back to their island to make sure Morgan was still imprisoned there. He also wanted a look around the village to see if there was anything that he wanted to buy for himself, so they used their combined magical powers and transported themselves there. They ended up straight in the centre of the village. Merlin was curious.

Alternative Dimension 2

Max, Jack and Alison worked in one of the shops. Max was starting to calm down, now that he was back in a place he thought to be safe, so he stopped worrying about the taps, or his wand or anything else. Jack's images were still horrific, but he was also starting to feel a bit better, and Alison could talk without her speech being too fast.

Merlin asked if he could visit the shop they worked in, so they escorted him to it.

All of a sudden someone shouted out, "Merlin's here!"

Everyone in the village went over, asking for autographs. Realising what was going on, some of the village police surrounded Merlin and protected him from the crowd. They asked where he would like to go. Merlin said that he was told of a magic shop where the three humans worked, and that he would like to visit it.

"Which shop is that?" the head officer asked (green skin, purple eyes, wore the police uniform).

"Ronnies," Merlin replied.

They helped him to the shop. Merlin thanked them, and entered the shop.

Inside, Ronnie (yellow ears, brown eyes, white skin on his face, a blue fur body, green wings, reptile skin on the arms) got down on one knee and asked how he may help.

Merlin asked straight out, "Do you sell books on black magic?"

Ronnie pretended to look shocked.

"Black magic? The idea that I could sell something so powerful shocks me."

Max explained, "We have already told him that you lie about selling black magic."

TR Eden

Merlin pointed out that he was not here to judge Ronnie, but that he desperately needed a particular book on black magic.

Ronnie escorted Merlin into the back of the shop and said, "The darkest books I have are through that wall."

Merlin smiled. "I see that is a fake wall, created by magic. You just walk through."

"Correct," Ronnie replied.

Inside the hidden room, Merlin could not believe his eyes. There were books here that were so ancient and powerful, that if they fell into the wrong hands they could do a lot of damage.

Merlin explained what he was looking for. He wanted a book on how someone reacts whilst under the control of someone else.

"Why do you want that book?" Jack asked.

"It's simple," Merlin replied, "I suspect Morgan has a spy in Camelot, and I need to find out who. The only way I can do this is if I know what to look for."

Ronnie went to the very back of the store and pulled out a book covered in cobwebs and dust. He smiled.

"I think this is what you are looking for."

Merlin suddenly realised he had no credits to pay for the book. He explained this to Ronnie.

"Is there any other way I can pay for it?" he asked.

Ronnie smiled. "If you sign 50 copies of your books I will give it to you."

Merlin took the deal.

Alternative Dimension 2

By now the group were getting hungry, so they headed back to the school where the chosen ones had served extra portions of the magical substance.

Merlin sat down and asked, "When is the food going to get here?"

Jack smiled; it had already arrived.

"You are a sorcerer. Just imagine what you would like to eat and it will appear in front of you."

Merlin tried, but he was so powerful that he made every meal in the room the same food.

As the dragons headed off to the school to rescue Morgan, she was preparing a plan to gain entry into Camelot. But this could only be done after she was released. The dragons flew down over the island. Mr Shaw asked Merlin what was going on.

Merlin replied, "They must have been called by her."

Max was starting to pace up-and-down saying, "I have forgotten something, I know I have forgotten something."

Alison was so scared she could hardly talk, and all Jack could see was a terrible death.

Merlin told the students that dragons were trustworthy creatures, which only attack if necessary.

A few minutes later a massive dragon landed in the village, just outside the school. As he started to speak, the windows of the building began to rattle because of the strength of his voice.

"What can we do for you?" Merlin asked.

The dragon smiled. "The prisoner, Morgan. We want her released."

TR Eden

Merlin pointed out that they could not do that, now that she knew where the shield was. It was Arthur's orders that she remained.

The dragon replied in a stern voice, "Why are you following the orders of Arthur, son of Uther, the magic slayer? The person who believed all magic was evil, including white magic that protects rather than destroys. He banished my people to an island just off the north coast. Morgan has promised us our land back if she claims the thrones of both Camelot and the Other-land."

Merlin pointed out that, in this case, she would have total power with the resources of both kingdoms, and would then be able to invade and conquer all the other small kingdoms.

The dragon replied, "We will have to take the risk. We can't trust Arthur or his servants, no matter how powerful they are. Arthur only trusts you because he knows you. If he did not, and you were a complete stranger, do you really think he would treat you the same way? Now, are you going to hand her over or not?"

Merlin replied in a powerful voice, "No. We can't risk it."

The lead dragon took off from the grounds and joined the first wave. There were three dragons; the first had a green, reptile-skin body with red patterns on the wings and was 8ft tall, the second also had a green, reptile body, but with yellow wings and was 7ft9 tall, the third was their leader, with a green, reptile body and green wings edged with gold. Everyone was scared at this point. After all, we all get scared from time-to-time.

The dragons flew down low and breathed a fireball, which set fire to the grounds.

The dragon started to speak, and said, "If you surrender Morgan, we will spare your island. As you posses magic we do not want to attack."

Alternative Dimension 2

He repeated himself again, as they did not want bloodshed. He then realised they had to attack. The chosen-ones stood outside the school and pointed their wands at the dragons.

"Freezzeo", they shouted, which was the ultimate ice spell. Two of the dragons' wings started to freeze.

The dragon Lord, who was watching the battle through the eyes of the lead dragon, ordered the second wave. The lead dragon ordered the next group of dragons to melt the ice of the wings of the first wave.

Merlin performed a communication spell, using the combined magical energy of the entire school. He pointed out that Arthur knew he was a sorcerer, and he accepted him.

The dragon Lord responded, "That was partly because you were friends with his father, which means you worked for Uther, making you a traitor."

Merlin responded, "Whilst I worked for Uther, I did my best to make sure that he did not push things too hard, by offering another point of view. If Uther had carried out his original objective, you would have been destroyed, instead of being banished to a small island."

The dragon Lord said, "Even if that were true, how can we trust Arthur?"

"What makes you think you can trust Morgan?"

The dragon responded in a loud voice, "Because she possesses magic."

Max was trying to remember what he had forgotten to do because the sense of worrying was overwhelming. Alison could not speak she was so anxious, and Jack kept on visualising their deaths.

Then Max clicked his fingers. "Why don't we use living metal to stop them?"

TR Eden

Derek said, "That is a nice plan in theory, but the dragons are not acting out of controlled magic, they are thinking for themselves, so there is no control magic to break."

The dragons flew over again and torched the rest of the village. All the magical wizards performed a shield spell over the village and the school. The dragon Lord told his troops to focus all their fire on one part of the school. They did this. The heat was so intense the wizards found it almost impossible to keep the shield up. Their powers were breaking under the hot air. In the end they had to drop the shield spell.

The dragon Lord said, "We have won! Now hand over Morgan."

The chosen ones ordered her release. The guards unlocked Morgan's prison cell and escorted her to the courtyard, where she thanked the dragon in their own tongue.

The dragon Lord said, "Because you posses magic we will not destroy your community. We will just escort Morgan to the Other-land."

The dragons took off and flew back north.

Alternative Dimension 2

Morgan's Love Plan

Back in the Other-land, the dragon Lord reminded Morgan of her promise to return their land back to them. Morgan knew that she had to posses both kingdoms and their assets. She needed a new plan to infiltrate Camelot. She went into her library to see if she could find a book which would help her.

Whilst looking through the books, she came across one about witchcraft, which she had acquired a long time ago. It was not uncommon for people who practiced black magic to have books on other types of magic, as it made them more powerful.

Arthur did not possess magic, as it was on Morgan's mother's side of the family. Because her mother had witch-blood in her, so did Morgan, but only in a quarter of her.

After sifting through the books, Morgan came across what she was looking for; a love-potion. If she transformed herself into a Princess, she would be able to marry Arthur, and then arrange a plot to kill him or imprison him for whatever charge she could think of. Morgan shouted out in a loud voice for Brittany.

Brittany came running into the libraries and asked, "What's the problem your ladyship?"

Morgan explained, "I want you to go out and collect the ingredients that I need to create this love potion."

She explained her plan to Brittany.

"Under Camelot law, if the King is killed and he has no children, the throne falls to the second in-line, which would be me as his Queen, or me as his sister. The people of Camelot would vote between the two positions but, as they are both me, I cannot lose."

Brittany agreed with her logic, and took her guard to help collect the ingredients. These included water from the enchanted mermaid lake, the hair from a giant bear (this variety of bear, existing only in this dimension, were 10 times the size of a polar bear), bats' wings from the giant bats (these also only existed in this dimension and were the size of lions), and finally dragon blood.

The party marched off to the enchanted lake. It would take about a day to travel there. Brittany had disguised her guards as market-sellers, travelling across the border to sell their products.

They came across a small village which was self-governing. They asked the village Chief if they could stay the night (the Chief was a giant, 7ft tall, blond hair, blue eyes, wore decorative armour with lots of badges on it). The Chief did not realise that they were in fact troops from another Kingdom. He agreed to let them stay till dawn.

The next morning they left the village and got back on their journey. Five hours later they reached the lake. When they got there, they could not believe their eyes. The mermaids and mermen were swimming up and down like dolphins. They were so graceful. Brittany asked if she could speak with someone in charge.

The water started to ripple and, all of a sudden, a giant head penetrated the water. The Mer-King was well built (blond hair, purple eyes, humanoid top, fish at the bottom, wore a crown made out of coral, had a gold sash). He asked what they wanted.

Brittany explained that they needed a cup of water from the lake.

The Mer-King said, "Do you know what you are asking for? This water is enchanted. It's a magical amplifier. If you use it in a potion it will make it ten-times more powerful. Why do you need it?"

Brittany explained that Morgan needed it to take the Throne of Camelot out of the hands of Arthur.

Alternative Dimension 2

The Mer-King responded. "I hear Arthur is not as bad as his father."

Brittany made him a promise.

"If you give us this water, Morgan will restore all the rights and traditions that existed before Uther took the throne."

"Very well", the Mer-King said.

He reached down and pulled out a golden cup, filled it up with water, and gave it to Brittany.

"I will trust you to fulfil your promise," he said, before he went back underwater.

Brittany and her guard started their march towards the deep forest kingdom, where the bears live. Brittany knew it would be extremely difficult to get close enough to get the hair sample, without the giant bear attacking them.

Brittany spent the next two hours thinking about it. Then she had a brain wave. Why didn't she make a cage to catch the bear? The only problem of course, was that the bear would see the trap. After all, this type of bear was super intelligent.

She decided to use her communication stone and speak to Morgan, to see if there was some sort of magic she could perform which would help them to hide the trap. Morgan told Brittany she could perform invisibility magic to hide the cage.

"The only problem," Morgan said, "is that to do this I must use all my magical energy and concentration, and even then I can only make it last an hour."

Brittany and her troops set off to try and find bait for the trap. The question was fruit or meat? As they walked through the wood, they spotted a large family of bears, so they hid and watched them eat a dead dear. The bears were massive and they all looked different. There were brown, black, white, and mixed colours. It was quite clear that they were sociable animals; there were about fifteen of them altogether.

TR Eden

The group left the area as quietly as possible, staying hidden the whole time. On the way back, Brittany noticed a lot of birds circling above (they were massive, 6ft wide wing span, 5ft bodies, gold wings, black heads, brown bodies, sharp claws, bright orange beaks, green eyes). They had obviously just killed something, because the birds were fighting each other over the kill.

Brittany decided to steal their kill, as trying to catch an animal by tracking it would be a lot harder, and her troops wanted to leave the bears' territory as soon as possible.

Brittany asked for a volunteer to cause a distraction to draw the birds away. One of her troops (blond hair, blue eyes, wore Morgan's army's armour, 5ft 6 tall) fired an arrow from his bow. This hit the wing of the lead bird and they began their attack on him. Brittany told him to run into the dense woodland. The birds were so big they could not land there.

In the mean time, Brittany grabbed the body of the giant dear (7ft long with 4ft legs and a shiny brown coat). The birds circled the woodland for two hours, and then gave up, as they needed to land and rest.

The guard made it back to Brittany, who rewarded him with a gold coin. Brittany placed the dead animal into the trap and told Morgan they were ready for her magic. Morgan reminded them she could only manage this for an hour. She focused all her magical energy on to the trap and it disappeared. The group hid in the bushes and waited.

45 minutes passed and there was no sign of the bear. Then, all of a sudden, a bear arrived in the area of the trap. He sniffed the air and saw the pile of meat. He went over and started to eat.

Brittany yelled into her communication stone, "Morgan, close the trap as we can't get close enough."

All of a sudden the trap became visible. A second later it shut. Morgan explained that she could not do both types of magic at the same time.

Alternative Dimension 2

Brittany got the hair sample from the bear's back. It could not bite her because the trap was a tight fit, preventing the bear from turning around.

Back in her castle, Morgan felt weak after using so much energy. Brittany explained to her that they were going to need her to open the trap and perform transport magic to get them out of the bear's way.

"Very well," said Morgan, "but I can only transport you a couple of miles away, my powers are still weak."

"Where do we head to now?" Brittany asked.

All of a sudden, a map appeared in her hand, like their books. When she unfolded the map it produced a hologram of the person who drew it. Brittany looked at the map with shock. They had to cross through the dark villages of the Other-land. Brittany knew these villages performed black magic but, unlike Morgan who only wanted power, the villages also practiced dark methods of inflicting pain. The methods were extremely painful and drawn out, like in the Tower of London, although they did not kill their victims unless necessary.

"How do these people dress?" Brittany asked, using her communication stone.

"Black robes, black shoes, dyed black hair."

Brittany realised that there was no going around these villages, because the cave of the giant bats was on the edge of one.

As they approached the first village, Morgan told most of the troops to go around the villages. It would take an extra four days to reach the cave, but she knew that, if the whole army went through the village, they would be detected. So she ordered her ten best troops to escort her through the villages. Brittany and her troops were worried about what they might face.

TR Eden

When the party entered the village, it looked more like a town from the wild west of America. There were screams of pain coming in every direction. The residents approached. They were hump-backed with scars all over them.

"What should we do with them?" one asked.

The others smiled.

"How long do you think it would take them to die? We have kept people in pain for hundreds of years."

The leader said that they were his. He escorted the group to his house which was massive. When he got inside he clicked his fingers. His back straightened, his hair became blond, and his eyes green.

"Sorry about that", he said.

"Who are you?" Brittany asked.

"I am Merlin's cousin," he replied.

Brittany was confused. If he knew Merlin then he must know that they were enemies.

"What's your name anyway?" she asked.

He smiled.

"Merlock. And if you want to know why I helped you, I don't care about your battle with Camelot. You needed help and I helped you. I hate anyone being torched so I pretend that I am one of them. Instead of killing or torturing people, I transport them to safety, so it looks like I have disposed of them. They will find no trace of the magic I use. Where would you like to be transported to?"

She smiled. "The giant bat cave on the other side of these villages."

"Very well," said Merlock, then performed the sorcery.

Alternative Dimension 2

All of sudden they came across the bat cave, imbedded into a massive mountain. The giant cave only existed in this dimension. It must have been 20ft wide and 15ft tall. It certainly lived up to the name!

As they slowly entered the cave, Brittany sent one of her people ahead to scout the cave and make sure it was safe, before she sent the rest of her group into a weak spot that may collapse on top of them.

The scout gave a shout, "It's ok. The cave is strong enough and the giant bats are asleep."

This did not surprise Brittany, as it was lunchtime and bats are nocturnal. On the floor was a pile of bones. Although these bats had been known to eat humans, they preferred horse meat.

One of the bats was waking-up after hearing their footsteps. After all, a bat's hearing is exceptionally acute.

Brittany started to wonder what to do next, until one of her troops whispered, "Get over here now."

Lying on the floor was a bat that looked like it had died from old-age. But more importantly its wings were still attached, so Brittany's troops grabbed the wings and crept out of the cave quietly so as to not disturb the other bats.

After they had left, the bats that were waking up went back to sleep. Brittany then used her communication stone to talk to the rest of her army, telling them where to meet up and regroup.

They then started on the long march back to the Other-land. It was a long trip because they did not dare enter the kingdom of Camelot, so they marched around it to avoid it.

When they finally got back to Morgan's castle, they went to hand her the ingredients. But a guard on the door said that she was meeting an important guest and could not be disturbed.

Morgan was meeting with the dragon Lord to request some dragon blood. She explained her plan to use a love potion to help secure the throne of Camelot, and that she needed dragon's blood. The dragon Lord reminded her of her promise about the land she owed them for their help. Morgan said that she intended to keep that promise.

"Very well," the dragon Lord said, "here is your blood sample".

"Do you want me to collect it?" Morgan asked.

"No, I can do this for myself," he replied. He picked up the needle which was on the table next to them, and took the blood sample. He handed it to Morgan.

"Good luck," he said, "for all our sakes."

Morgan collected the other ingredients from Brittany, and brewed the potion. When the potion was ready, she started on the second part of her plan. To use it to get the throne of Camelot!

Alternative Dimension 2

Use of the Love Potion

Morgan headed down from the Other-land. She used transformation magic so that no-one would be able to recognise her. She was going to claim that she was a Princess from one of the islands at the top of the country. She knew that Arthur would not be able to doubt her story, because he had never been that far north, as it was where Uther banished all the magical creatures from his realm. Brittany wanted to come as well, but Morgan knew she did not have enough energy to transform her appearance. They marched from Morgan's castle down into England. They were not stopped because they looked like genuine royal visitors.

That night, Morgan needed to see what was going on, so she used her servant Sir Emtoro. He was standing in a room with the other Knights. Arthur shouted out that he wanted to find a bride, so that he could become a father to the next Prince or Princess of Camelot.

After a long journey south, Morgan finally reached Camelot. She had decided not to use transport magic in case someone saw her, and warned Arthur that a powerful sorcerer was approaching his Kingdom.

"Open the gates," her guard yelled out to the gatekeeper. "Princess Casy wishes to meet the King!"

Arthur heard the shouting from his bed chamber.

"What is all the shouting about?" he called.

The guard yelled, "There is a Princess Casy".

Princess Casy was, of course, Morgan in disguise. She looked beautiful (long blonde hair, sky blue eyes, pale face, wore a dress that was made out of gold, she was not too tall at only 5ft12).

Arthur shouted out to his guard, "Let her in, so she can present herself."

TR Eden

As she entered the castle, a sharp chill went down the spines of the students, especially Max, Jack and Alison. They told Merlin that they sensed something evil quite close by. Merlin said he felt it too. It upset our three heroes to the point where their feelings of anxiety were boiling over like a kettle.

Alison could hardly speak, all she managed to say was "What do you think is wrong?"

Max started pacing up-and-down, but making sure that he stood on the same paving slabs over and over again. Jack kept on visualising their deaths.

Merlin replied to Alison, "I definitely think something evil is close by."

Meanwhile Morgan/Casy was being escorted to King Arthur's throne room. She got down on one knee.

"My Lord," she said.

She knew Arthur would make her rise up from the floor by holding her hand and kissing it. What Arthur did not know, however, was that the love potion worked by touch. As soon as Arthur touched her hand, he would be in love.

And indeed that's what happened, because, ten seconds later, Arthur got down on one knee and proposed to Casy/Morgan. The whole court went into shock. They could hardly believe that Arthur would be so rash.

When he got up again, a guard shouted out "God save the King!" and clapped. And so did everyone else.

Inside the royal apartments, Arthur told Merlin to arrange the wedding to take place straight away. Merlin replied that this would be difficult to organise. He was lying through his teeth. If he used his magic, the wedding could take place in about twelve hours time, but he wanted to stall for time to work on a plan to make the King see sense.

Alternative Dimension 2

So Merlin proposed a compromise. "I will have it organised for two days time. In the meanwhile, why don't you take your new fiancée on a tour of your Kingdom?"

"What a great idea," Arthur said.

He then decided the best way to start the tour was to have a banquet in the great hall that evening, to show off his fiancée to the court.

Arthur requested that Merlin should come to his apartments to chat about the wedding plans. Merlin went into great detail about the ceremony. Arthur looked impressed by the amount of detail he had gone to. Merlin had explained the ceremony would be a mixture of tradition and creation - this would be the part that was created just for Arthur and his bride.

Merlin felt a vibration in his pocket. It was his communication stone.

Merlin asked Arthur, "Is there anything else I can do for you?"

Arthur smiled at his old friend and said, "No, you may leave now."

Merlin bowed his head and left the room.

Merlin walked for about five minutes through the corridors of the castle, until he found an empty room. He went inside, got out his communication stone and asked it "What's the problem?"

Mr Underwood started to express his concerns about the future Queen.

Merlin whispered, "So we need to meet up? Why don't you come to my apartment in the north tower?"

The group of students were worn out from the stairs and were trying to catch their breath.

TR Eden

Meanwhile Merlin had beaten them there by using levitation magic. Arthur now knew he was a white sorcerer, so he would not get into trouble.

Merlin said, "It's obvious that the Princess has seduced Arthur by magic, and because I can't detect it, it's a potion-based spell. But how could she create such a spell that would be strong enough to overcome the entire court? She must have used an amplifying ingredient."

Merlin clicked his fingers. "She has used dragon blood!"

Mr Underwood asked, "What is dragon blood?"

Merlin explained. "It's a magical enhancer, which increases the strength of a potion by 100%."

Max, Jack and Alison suddenly froze to the spot. They could feel the presence of basic witch-craft. They told Mr Underwood who was shocked. How could they sense something that Merlin could not?

Merlin interrupted by saying, "Awareness of magic is an individual thing. They must have a trace of witch-blood inside them."

The three heroes shook with fear.

Alison asked, in a very scared voice, "Does that mean we are needed again?"

Merlin nodded. "I am afraid so. We are going to need your touch of witch-craft to increase the power of the energy beam that will break the dragon-blood enchanted potion."

"How do we do that?" Mr Underwood asked.

Merlin pointed out that he did not posses enough energy by himself, so he wanted the strength of the students and Mr Underwood to help generate the energy needed.

Alternative Dimension 2

Merlin continued, "What I want is for the students to transmit their energy to you Mr Underwood, who will then pass it on to me. The students will point their wands at you, and you will point your wand at me. All you have to do is shout out *Transform*."

The energy shot out of the students' wands as a bolt of blue light. They all focused on Mr Underwood, who then channelled a bolt of blue light into Merlin. Merlin's wand shot out a bolt of energy so strong that he went flying backwards across the room. The others gathered around him, asking if he was ok.

Merlin smiled. "At least we know it works."

The tour of the kingdom went down well with the subjects. They visited ten villages and towns, where all the citizens shouted out "God save the King and the Princess!"

Then, after two days, they headed back to Camelot for the wedding feast. The meal was going to be incredible. It was a twenty course banquet.

During the meal, everyone raised their glasses and toasted the Princess. One of the knights shouted out, "God save Camelot!"

There was a huge cheer, then, under the traditions of Camelot, the Princess and her ladies left the room and allowed the knights to get drunk with their King. Arthur spent the rest of the evening describing why he liked his future bride.

Merlin and the students were worried about the wedding, because if Arthur went through with it, he would probably be killed so that the throne would pass to the second-in-line.

TR Eden

The Day of the Wedding

It was the day of the wedding and Morgan, who was still pretending to be a Princess from another kingdom, was talking to her royal household. These were servants that Arthur had given her as a pre-wedding gift.

One of the maids commented on Morgan's future husband, saying "What a handsome King he is. And he has been on many quests, like the hunt for the sword-in-the- stone."

Morgan smiled through gritted teeth. She hated being reminded of Arthur's achievements.

Meanwhile, back in the King's apartments, Merlin was acting as man-servant to Arthur. This was a very privileged position, because it meant Arthur could confide in him his true feelings and problems. It was about 9 o'clock in the morning, and Arthur was getting washed and changed. When he was decent, he called Merlin into the royal chamber. This was effectively his bedroom.

Merlin played along with his fantasy of the Princess, by saying "She is very pretty."

Arthur nodded. "She is the most beautiful woman I have ever seen."

Merlin could still sense the use of black magic within the Kingdom. He felt a cold sensation going down his back Merlin knew he had to act fast. So at the earliest opportunity he asked if he could be excused. He met Mr Underwood outside Arthur's apartments. Who asked Merlin to tell him about the ceremony. Merlin agreed.

"At midnight, the King will leave the main castle and head to the betrothal palace."

The betrothal palace was a special building. It only had four rooms, but they were covered in gold and bright tapestries.

Alternative Dimension 2

"Meanwhile, the Queen moves to a palace which is decorated in the same way as Arthurs. Each palace is exactly four miles away from the bell tower. When the bell strikes twelve for midday, both parties ride to the bell tower. At the front of the bell tower there are two doors, both with a gold frame. One is labelled 'For the true and just leader of Camelot'. The other says 'The gracious future Queen and her beloved King'. They go through these doors and then the service will begin. The royal band will sound a fanfare, and then the guests will enter. They will bow before the future Queen and their beloved King, then take their seats.

"The last person to enter will be the ceremony master, who will oversee the wedding. He will walk until he comes across a gold star in the dead centre of the room. He will get down on one knee, then stand up and conduct the service." Merlin smiled. "This means that when we use the detection magic, everyone will be concentrating on his speech."

Max, Jack and Alison felt uneasy about this plan. They were worried that Arthur would realise they had magical powers. Merlin did his best to reassure them.

"Whoever the person who is using back magic, they won't attack you. They cannot run the risk that they would be detected by me. I would then tell Arthur, and that person would go to prison."

It was the day of the wedding, and everything was happening in the way that Merlin had described. With King Arthur and his prospective bride leaving their traditional dwellings, they marched towards the bell tower. The masses applauded and shouted until their throats became sore.

When they reached the bell tower, the couple were kept away from each other, so that Arthur would enter exactly one minute after Morgan. As Morgan entered the building, Arthur's closest servants were standing directly in front of it.

"This is a great day," the servants said.

TR Eden

Morgan entered the room and sat down on her throne. A minute later Arthur joined her. Arthur then summoned the Chief Guard. This was the most senior member of Arthur's army (6ft 2 inches, blond hair, brown eyes, wore a uniform made from red and gold thread).

"How may I serve you?" he asked.

Arthur said, "It's time to open the central doors."

The Chief Guard pushed as hard as he could, and slowly the doors crept open. The first well-wishers entered. They presented themselves to the royal couple, by getting down on one knee or bowing in front of them. They then took their seats.

The final party to enter was Princess Jade's court. She was about to acknowledge by bowing, when Arthur ordered her to stop.

"You are a ruler in your own right, which makes you my equal."

The rest of her court or school friends bowed, and sat down.

Then there were five knocks on the door. Two guards entered, shouting out, "Make way for the Master of ceremonies."

The Master entered (short, about 5ft, long grey beard, wore the robes of office which were made out of gold and silver, on his chest was a red eagle which symbolised knowledge) and got down on one knee.

"My respects," he said.

As the service started, Merlin winked at Mr Underwood, which meant he was ready. Mr Underwood told his students to keep their wands hidden underneath their clothing, but to point them at him and concentrate on transferring energy directly to him. Mr Underwood then pointed his wand secretly at Merlin.

Alternative Dimension 2

When they performed the spell, a massive amount of energy was channelled into Mr Underwood, who then transferred it to Merlin. A bolt of energy shot out of Merlin's wand. It was so powerful he flew backwards! The magical beam swirled around the room, before hitting Morgan, which broke her love potion and transformation magic, and she suddenly appeared as Arthur's sister.

Merlin turned away, thinking that was the only source of black magic in the court. But then the beam hit Sir Emtoro.

Arthur ordered their immediate arrest, but Morgan had planned a safe transport spell route back to her Kingdom. She grabbed Sir Emtoro's hand and they vanished before the courts' eyes.

Mr Underwood was shocked.

He asked Merlin, "How could someone have enough mental energy to perform the transport spell for that distance?"

Merlin said, "There is an old piece of magic. If you are a sorcerer, you can enchant an object and then use it as a marker, so when you perform transport magic you will return to that object."

TR Eden

Merlin's Dream

That night, Merlin was woken by a scene from the future. It was terrifying. It was also vague in places, with little detail on what the people looked like. But there was enough to worry even him. He had a cold feeling running down his back.

Being a sorcerer, he often had dreams about the future. He had seen an attack on the island by a Roman army that was ten times stronger than the entire population put together. It looked like there could be as many as 50,000 troops ready for the first attack on Britain. He was so worried he ran down the stairs and headed for Arthur's bed chamber.

Outside Arthur's private rooms there were two guards who stopped him from entering. They told him that the King was asleep and did not want to be disturbed.

Arthur heard the voice of his old friend and said, "Let him in."

Merlin told Arthur about his dream. Arthur knew that the island had lots of metal resources that the Romans might be interested in. He also knew to trust Merlin's visions.

Meanwhile, across the sea in France, the Roman Emperor had arrived at camp to discuss the invasion of the island with two of his generals. They decided to attack in two weeks time, as it would take that long for them to assemble their troops from all over Europe.

The Emperor smiled.

"Good," he said, "the sooner we have their mineral supplies the better."

Meanwhile, back in Camelot, Merlin was talking to the students about his dream of the Roman invasion.

Max pointed out in a shaky voice, "According to our history, the Romans did not invade at this time."

Alternative Dimension 2

Mr Underwood pointed out that they were in a different dimension, so things were slightly different.

Jack's head was full of vile images of war; images of people being stabbed and worse were rushing around inside his head. Alison had become so anxious she could hardly talk. Max, although he was able to ask questions, was pacing up-and-down in the room, thinking that his wand would break and leave him defenceless.

The rest of the students tried to reassure them, except for Prex, who spat, as he hated Max, Jack and Alison. Given how severe the situation was, Arthur used Merlin, who used a piece of communication magic to summon any leader that was interested in the shield to come to Camelot. He knew it would probably take three days for them to arrive.

In the meantime, Arthur asked two trusted knights, Sir Lancelot and Sir Gawain, to drill his troops, so that they would be up to the standard expected by the royal guests. The castle was cleaned from top-to-bottom.

It was three days later, and the guests had arrived at Camelot to discus Merlin's visions of an invasion. There were ten leaders altogether, all in charge of their own kingdoms. Some of the kingdoms were the size of a small town; others were large pieces of land.

The only person not there was Morgan. She was afraid that, if she returned to Camelot, Merlin would find some way of holding her captive.

The names of the nine leaders were: King Brandon (5ft 11, blond hair, green eyes, wore royal armour with a picture of a swan on it, as this was his badge), King John (6ft, black hair, brown eyes, wore armour showing a picture of an eagle) Lord Mastereoro (6ft ginger hair,6ft1, blue eyes, wore armour showing a picture of wolf), Queen Stephanie (brown hair, 5ft 9, blue eyes, wore armour showing a picture of a bear), Emperor Neilton (6ft 4, black hair, green eyes, wore armour showing a picture of a snake), Queen Amy (black hair, 5ft 9, blue eyes, wore armour showing a picture of a tiger), King Melton (6ft, black hair, green eyes, wore armour showing a picture of a panther), Prince Hanckton (5ft 10, blond hair with a touch of grey, wore amour showing a picture of a crow), Princess Melanie (6ft, brown hair, green eyes, wore amour showing a picture of a falcon), and the last major land owner was of cause Morgan.

After hearing about the love potion and her plan to take the throne, the leaders realised that Morgan was not to be trusted.

Arthur invited the leaders into the debating chamber. This was a massive room and, in the centre, there was the fabled round table of Camelot, where the King and his knights would sit.

Arthur explained, "Although I am in charge, I like to make sure that I am approachable, and when we sit at this table we are all equal. Now please sit."

Lord Mastereoro started off the debate, saying "We need to know exactly what Merlin saw in his vision."

So Arthur sent for his friend to join them. Merlin entered the doorway and got down on one knee. Arthur smiled.

"Arise my old friend," he said.

Arthur then asked him exactly what he had seen. Merlin closed his eyes and started to think.

"It was the most horrific thing I had ever seen. There were dead bodies lying on the floor where they had been attacked by sword and arrow. Camelot and the other kingdoms were in flames; the Romans had captured the survivors and taken them back to Rome to become slaves."

Lord Mastereoro asked, "If Morgan's kingdom is attacked, would she then be allowed to join this council?"

Arthur smiled. "That goes without saying."

Alternative Dimension 2

Merlin pointed out that they might have an object that could protect the kingdoms.

"The shield of Excalibur. I recommend that Arthur has the shield."

King John protested, "Why should he have the shield? I am a far better fighter than he is."

Merlin pointed out that, the only way the magic works is if everyone is united behind one leader.

Arthur then suggested, "Why don't we have a tournament for the shield?"

TR Eden

The Tournament for the Shield

On the day of the tournament, Arthur had arranged to have his suit of armour cleaned by his servants. He was busy practicing sword fighting. He was confident that he would win. After an hour-and-a-half of practice, the other people fighting summoned Arthur, so that they could decide on a judge for the contest.

King Brandon was quite keen that it should be a respectable person, with knowledge of the traditions for such an important contest. He made it quite clear it had to be a noble contest. He smiled.

"What about Merlin?"

Queen Stephanie disagreed, "He was too close to Arthur. We need someone of royal blood who would be completely impartial. What about Princess Jade and her court?"

"Very well," they all agreed.

Merlin then explained that he had put all their names into a hat, and that he would pick them out to decide who was fighting whom.

The first pair to be drawn was King Brandon and Queen Stephanie. They demonstrated a great deal of skill and strength. The rule was simple; the first person to draw blood from their opponent would win the contest.

As the battle continued for an hour-and-a-half, both people were becoming tired. As the battle raged on, Merlin spoke to Mr Underwood and his students.

"Whatever happens," he said, "Arthur must win the shield so that he can use its full power and then pass it on to you. I suggest that we use magic to make sure that Arthur wins."

Mr Underwood was shocked.

Alternative Dimension 2

"If we get caught we will be charged with high treason by the other Royals fighting."

Merlin sighed. "It's the only way the shield can end up in your possession, so that it never falls into the hands of someone evil."

They all agreed it was the only way. The battle continued until Queen Stephanie cut King Brandon's leg. She was declared the winner.

Next to fight was King John against King Arthur. Merlin looked nervous as the two Kings entered the battle arena. He knew that Arthur would have to win so he could take ownership of the shield, so Merlin created a distraction field around King John, causing him to lose his balance. King John collapsed on the floor, King Arthur then cut his arm and was declared the winner.

The final contest was archery between King Arthur and Queen Stephanie. As ladies always went first in such contests, Queen Stephanie took the first shot and got a bull's eye.

Then it was Arthur's turn. He took his first shot and also got a bull's eye. Sir Gawain noticed that Merlin had his eyes closed and was whispering enchantments. He was horrified that he was helping Arthur to cheat, but did not say anything because he wanted Arthur to win.

On her second shot, Queen Stephanie hit the outer ring and scored twenty five points, whereas Arthur, thanks to Merlin directing the arrow, got another bull's eye. He was declared the winner, and temporary leader of the island. He then asked Merlin how he could remove the shield from the stone.

Merlin smiled. "When the time is right I will tell you."

Because all the other leaders thought that Arthur had won fairly, they backed him up. Merlin felt guilty about rigging the contest, but knew that it had had to be done.

TR Eden

The Romans Invade

Inside the Roman camp , Caesar the 8th (wore the crown of the empire, his armour was made out of metal and coated in gold, he was 5ft 11, short blond hair, blue eyes) was drawing up a plan of attack. He had his two commanders with him; Brutus (6ft tall, short black hair, brown eyes, wore the best quality armour), and Nero (6ft 1, short black hair, blue eyes, also wore high quality armour). Out of curiosity they asked him about the plan of attack.

Creaser smiled. "We will attack on each side of England."

"How will we do that?" Nero asked.

Creaser explained, "We will disguise our first wave of attack as trade ships."

The Romans traded in villages close to sea ports

Brutus asked, "Why are we going to invade?"

Creaser turned round and said, "In order for the Empire to survive, we need a vast quantity of minerals. England and the rest of that island have what we need."

Creaser continued to discuss the plan of attack.

"Our warships will follow on behind to provide support."

Brutus was worried. "The trade ships are not designed for battle and have very few weapons on board."

Creaser pointed out, "They do not have to be heavily armed if the ships slip unnoticed into the ports."

Back in Camelot, Merlin was troubled by the events that were occurring.

In the meantime, Arthur decided to go on a royal tour of some of the villages and communities. He was greeted by a huge cheer.

Alternative Dimension 2

Back inside the castle, Jack kept on visualising what it would be like to be a Roman slave, not being fed properly, being whipped to achieve a task, or worse, being sacrificed to a lion in the arena

Alison was so nervous that she couldn't speak, and Max was pacing up-and-down murmuring "I know I have forgotten something."

Mr Underwood tried to calm them down by promising to stay with them whatever happened. Jack pointed out that they had heard similar promises before back on earth in their dimension, and all his friends had died.

Mr Underwood asked Merlin, "How long is it until the Roman army reaches Camelot?"

Merlin said in a worried voice, "About forty eight hours, maybe less."

Jack said, "Let's head back to the ship. We will be safe there."

Mr Underwood said, "We have to help these people. After all, we are white magic wizards."

Merlin agreed, "It's our most basic law to help whenever we can."

Arthur returned from the tour of his Kingdom. He reported his success to Merlin.

"Everyone is behind us in our plan to fight the Romans," he said.

Merlin asked Arthur, "What about the lower kingdoms? Some of them are just farmers? They have no defences."

This was a difficult problem for Arthur. If he allowed the villages inside the castle, there wouldn't be enough room for everyone.

TR Eden

Merlin suggested, "Why not allow them to camp outside the castle and allow them to enter if needed?"

Arthur agreed, and suggested that all the other castles on the island did the same.

"But how will we get the message across? My messengers cannot travel across the whole island in forty eight hours?"

Merlin smiled. "If you allow me to use communication magic, I can tell everyone in one go."

Arthur agreed. However, being brought up by Uther, he had been taught that all magic was evil, so he was always slightly disturbed by its use.

Everyone heard the message inside their heads, and all villagers and farmers headed for their nearest inland castle. The farmers had picked their crops and transported them to the camps outside the castles.

At exactly 12 noon, the Roman forces boarded their ships. These were powered by slaves who were forced to row, even when they were exhausted. If they stopped for just a minute they would be whipped by massive horsewhips.

On the lead Galion, Creaser dispatched his final orders about how the invasion was going to take place, to his two commanders Nero and Brutus.

"All the troops inside the trade ships will land on the coastline at the same time. That way, when we invade, they can guard the coast and occupy the port until our warships arrive. When the whole army has landed on the island, we will advance in one go, as we will outnumber their armies. Their forces will weaken and eventually crumble. We will then capture the remaining solders and peasants, which we will take back to Rome and sell for a handsome profit."

The commanders agreed and started to rub their hands together.

Alternative Dimension 2

The first of the trade ships arrived off the coast of the island at 2.30pm and started to look around. The ports, to their surprise, were empty, and all the valuables had been taken. It was as if they knew that the Romans were coming.

Unaware that the ports were empty, Caesar, who was hiding in the sea mist, waited three hours before he landed, thinking that this should be enough time to secure the ports.

Eventually, Caesar gave the order to invade and, all of a sudden, all the gallons arrived in the port. When they arrived at the coast, they were shocked to see the place was deserted.

Caesar spoke to Nero, asking him, "How did they know we were going to invade?"

Nero said, "I suspect that it was someone who can see through the barriers of time. It could only be someone who possessed magic."

Caesar pointed out, "Someone with that much power would make an excellent slave."

Nero responded, "You would need to find some way to control his powers."

First, the army was restless that they had been promised a battle. They collected a commission on anything won in the fight instead of being paid wages. This was a very clever system which meant they would always fight to the best of their ability because they would collect more plunder.

Caesar marched his army from the coast inland. As they arrived in the farm area, they saw that all the food had been picked and again, the place was deserted. Caesar knew that he had to find some minerals as soon as possible to pay the troops, so they would not rebel.

In the meantime, twenty miles outside Camelot, Arthur had placed some spies to warn of the Roman invasion. Twenty

TR Eden

four hours had passed before the spies got to see the Roman army marching towards them.

They quickly rode back to Camelot shouting, "The Romans are coming! The Romans are coming!"

Arthur said to Merlin, "Here we go. Can you use your communication magic to warn all the other kingdoms?"

Arthur distrusted magic, but knew the only way to co-ordinate the defence was to use Merlin's abilities.

Within two hours, the Romans had surrounded the castle and started to fire a barrage of arrows at the walls. Merlin had secretly enchanted the castle, so their weapons had little effect. The only danger would be if the arrows came over the walls and hit Arthur's troops.

Merlin performed a piece of shield magic which encased the castle inside a force-field.

The other leaders were worried about their subjects, and themselves, becoming slaves.

Meanwhile, all the students were shaking with fear. After all, everyone suffers from fear when their lives are in danger. Max was so scared that, as he was pacing up-and-down, he was worried that he might do something that would endanger everyone else. Alison was so scared about becoming a Roman slave she could hardy move, and Jack kept on visualising life as a Roman slave being whipped and abused by his future masters.

Arthur walked into the courtyard to have a word with Merlin.

He asked "How do I become the united leader of the kingdoms and remove the shield from the stone?"

He tried to pull it out, but it remained fixed inside the stone. Merlin pointed out that, to remove the shield, you must have the support of every kingdom.

Alternative Dimension 2

"But I have that," Arthur replied.

"Not quite," Merlin said, "There is one kingdom that has not shown its allegiance to you; Morgan. You will have to get her to accept you as the temporary united leader."

Arthur asked his old friend Merlin, "How do we get to Morgan's kingdom? The castle is completely surrounded, and you need all your power to repel the attack."

"Simple," Merlin smiled, "by using the power of your sword Excalibur, my shield spell will last twelve hours."

Meanwhile, to protect the other castles on the island, Merlin had used up a lot of energy to protect them to the same level as Camelot.

"Why do we need the power of Excalibur to transport us? You have done this hundreds of times before," Arthur asked.

Merlin said, "Maintaining the shields takes alot of energy."

"What do I do now?"

"Hold the sword out."

Merlin touched the blade and it started to glow orange, and then flashed. It was so bright they closed their eyes.

When they opened them again, they were standing in some woodland. Mr Underwood took Arthur to one side and asked him what they would do if they came across any Romans?

Arthur pointed out, "Romans only attack big targets at first to fortify their position and take control. As we are only a small group, they should ignore us. Also it will be easy to spot patrols and hide, as they always advance in large numbers, banging their shields. There are only twenty three of us, so it should be easy to find hiding spaces."

To reach Morgan's castle, the group walked through deserted farms and villages. The group felt a bit sad, because people had been working in their land for hundreds of years, and here it was, completely abandoned.

After two days of walking, they finally reached the border. They were surprised to see that the Romans had not crossed the border. There was no sign of them. They also discovered two of Morgan's troops on guard, who asked what they wanted. They explained that they were there to see Morgan, as they needed her help.

The guards agreed to take them to Morgan, as long as they handed over their weapons. They agreed, but Arthur refused to hand over Excalibur because of its power, so one of the guards sent a messenger to Morgan, saying that he refused to hand over the sword.

She smiled and said, "That is to be expected. Very well, as he is my half-brother he can keep it."

The messenger ran back to the guard saying he could keep it.

Arthur said, "As your King I demand you obey me."

The guards burst out laughing.

"You are only our King when it suits you," they said, "It's Morgan who rules the country, and we are completely loyal to her."

Morgan sent a telepathic message to the guards, telling them to escort the party to the throne room.

When they arrived, they were all forced down on to their knees in front of the throne. Morgan entered and sat down on the throne.

"I have been looking forward to the day when you would come back to my castle. Now that all the guards are loyal to me, I can hold you here indefinitely."

Arthur began saying, "The Romans have invaded."

Alternative Dimension 2

Morgan smiled. "I know. I also know that they won't cross the border."

"How can you be sure?" Arthur asked.

Morgan replied, "Simple. I have my secret weapon, which is my allies, the dragons. They could breathe fire on the Romans, forcing them back."

"Do you know how many have invaded? Why don't you use your powers to look?"

Morgan looked into her crystal ball and was shocked by the size of the invading force. If they made it to her kingdom they would capture the people and turn them into slaves. She was so concerned that she used her dragon communication powers to summon one of the dragon leaders, and asked for advice.

The dragon thought about it, then pointed out to Morgan that she had little choice. Morgan reluctantly asked Arthur what she could do to help him and everyone else. She was so annoyed that she was grinding her teeth as she said it, and was clenching the arms of her throne.

Arthur explained, "As you are probably aware, I cannot activate the shield unless all the affected kingdoms accept me as their leader."

At the same time, Merlin was preparing himself. He knew they would need his help to activate the shield.

Morgan repeated, "I have to express my allegiance to you as the true King?"

The words stuck in her throat. In the end, she knew she had no choice. So she took a big breath and said,

"I swear my allegiance to you, Arthur, King of the united realms."

TR Eden

The shield started to glow bright orange, but then stopped. Arthur asked Merlin what was wrong.

Merlin replied, "It needs some magical energy to activate it."

Merlin and Morgan concentrated their full powers on it, but this still was not enough. Arthur collapsed to the floor.

"My father's quest to rid all the kingdoms of magic has resulted in the total defeat of our kingdoms," he said.

Morgan said, "Not quite. There is always Princess Jade and her court."

Merlin looked shocked.

"How did you know that they posses magical abilities?"

Morgan smiled. "I have known for ages."

Arthur turned to Merlin, asking him, "Is this true? You kept this information away from me?"

Merlin replied, "Yes. I was protecting them from your father."

Arthur asked, "Why didn't you tell me after he died?"

"Because I was concerned that you might imprison them for possessing magic. After all, you trust me because you know me, but you don't know them or what they might me capable of."

"Very well," Morgan said, "Whilst this is a most interesting conversation, the Romans are in the process of ransacking the island."

So Merlin took Mr Underwood to one side and told him, "The students must channel their energy into you, and you do the same to me. I will project on to the shield."

The students used a transference spell to channel the energy into Mr Underwood, who then channelled it on to

Alternative Dimension 2

Merlin, who released it on to the shield. There was a massive blast of energy. Mr Underwood channelled the energy onto Merlin, who found it impossible to control the beam of energy, so he went flying backwards.

All of a sudden, the shield started to glow bright red. The shield released an explosion of energy which was like a bright yellow light.

All of a sudden, the humans of the island had what could only be described as force fields around them. But this was only the humans and those in human form. It did not work on non-human members of the island, so Merlin told them not to get involved. The Roman weapons just bounced off the citizens of the temporary united country. The Romans took the only option left, which was to turn around and run back to the coast. The people of the island cheered and applauded.

Two days later, Arthur held a banquet to celebrate their great victory. All the island's leaders attended, including Morgan. At the banquet, Arthur officially handed back control to the veracious leaders. They then had a problem; what to do with the shield?

All the leaders wanted it.

Prince Edmond said, "Although I respect Arthur as a leader, I can't allow him to keep such a powerful object that one day might be a weapon. And as Merlin knows how to activate the shield, he may find a way to use it just for himself. Magical powers run in the family, just look at how powerful his half-sister Morgan is."

Prince Arran said, "Are you suggesting that you should have it?"

Edmond and Arran had been arguing over their kingdom boundaries for decades. Merlin asked if he could speak.

TR Eden

"I think I have a solution. What if you give it to me? I know how to destroy it. I also do not have any land or titles to protect."

"How will you destroy it?" they asked.

Merlin replied, "Simple. On Princess Jade's island there is a volcano which contains dragon's breath. If we throw the shield into it, the shield will burn up."

"How can we trust you?" the others asked.

Merlin pointed out that they had little choice.

"If someone learns how to tap the power of the shield, then their family will be rulers forever. No-one would be able to attack them, and there are other powers in the shield which have not been used yet."

The leaders agreed and handed the shield to Merlin.

Alternative Dimension 2

The Final Part: After the Battle

King Arthur decided to help and protect Merlin on his journey to the island. He was acting on behalf of the other leaders, who wanted to make sure that the shield wasn't stolen by anyone. As they marched through the villages, some people, who were returning back to their homes after staying protected within castles and forts, cheered Arthur and his guard. They decided to camp close to one of those villages.

When they arrived in the village of Nonston, some ladies came running up to them, handing them gifts, such as necklaces and rings made out of pure gold and decorated with precious stones. The village leader (short black hair, blue eyes, 5ft 11, wore a smart orange dress) stated how relived they felt.

Mr Underwood said, "Good. We have nearly completed our mission to get the shield for Devena."

After marching for three days, the party finally reached the coastline. Merlin took Arthur to one side. He knew it was time to tell the truth about Princess Jade and her court; the fact that they were wizards.

After Merlin had told him, Arthur took a step backwards and then yelled at his friend, "Why didn't you tell me?"

Merlin told his friend to calm down. He made it very clear that he had wanted to tell him for months, but that he was unsure as to how he would react to the news.

"Also, your father persecuted people who could perform magic," he said.

The following morning, Merlin told Arthur he would have to leave his troops behind. Merlin claimed the people of the island did not like the idea of being invaded by hundreds of troops that would outnumber their population

Arthur said, "Very well, I trust you old friend, so I will do what you ask and go there alone."

TR Eden

After breakfast, Arthur, Merlin and the students crossed over to the island. When they got there, Mr Underwood used his communication stone to talk to the chosen ones, and asked them to drop the camouflage spell they had been using to disguise them.

"Very well," Abby said.

All of a sudden, Arthur was surrounded by aliens. The shock of seeing them was so great that he passed out. When he came round, Merlin told him to take it easy.
"You are not imaging this," he said, "These people want to take the shield to another dimension to help a witch Queen."

Arthur was escorted to a private chamber where he talked with the chosen ones for over two hours. They agreed that Arthur would hand the shield over to them, as long as they promised never to return to the dimension again.

After Arthur had handed over the shield, Merlin took Arthur back to the mainland, and wiped his memory of everything that had happened. Merlin made him think he had dreamt it all. He also imprinted images of the shield being destroyed, so that Arthur would assume he had carried out his mission. Arthur came round.

"I remembered we destroyed the shield! It's over," Arthur said.

Merlin nodded. "Of course we did".

Back on the ship, everyone was rushing around to prepare for takeoff. Derek asked the chosen ones to perform a piece of invisibility magic, so it looked like the island was covered in a thick sea-fog. The island transformed back into a spaceship. Devena then made contact using her crystal ball, and arranged an agreed place to hand over the shield in safety.

Alternative Dimension 2

When the ship arrived there, she took the shield from them and thanked them for all their efforts. Derek said if she needed any help in the future she just had to ask for it.

After everyone was on board, the ship it left for its new destination.

Lightning Source UK Ltd.
Milton Keynes UK
UKOW03f1152100117
291741UK00001B/54/P